High Shelf

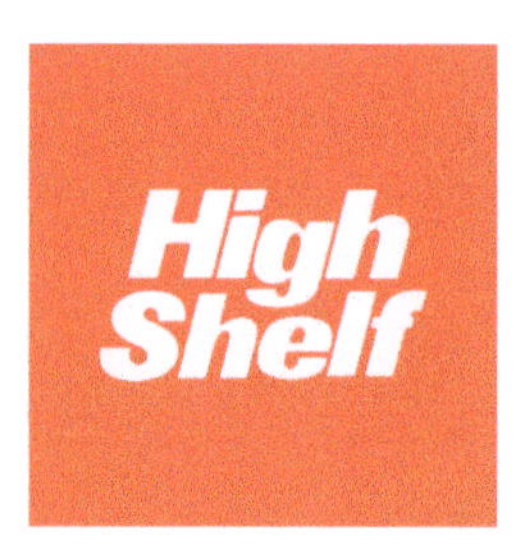

High Shelf Issue VIII 3.9.19
Portland, Oregon.
Copyright 2019, High Shelf Press

ISBN: 978-1-7330279-6-0

Cover Image by Jodie Filan
Design and Layout by C. M. Tollefson
Edited by Angela Dribben & C. M. Tollefson

High Shelf IX

August 2019

"...Boxes filled, new home needs
but no new home for that
bastard of a man left her
not at the altar but
in the recovery room..."

Laura Lee

"... The space between what was and what will be stretched thin and translucent, like a secret whispered in the dark. Rings in my trunk mark time with echoes reverberating..."

Niku Rice

Table Of Contents

Poetry, Poetry Not

Marek Kulig

Poetry is not some asshole — okay,
it's not gonna stiff you with two-fifty
when it owes you the whole three.

What it will do is
it'll hand over the last half dollar
in a fist full of mixed change.

suck on this

Megan Russell

Saxophones are amber glazed city lights finally giving into the first muffled sob,
       sheets crammed in fist crammed in pink wet mouth,
Crying *pink/wet*
about some sick boy who smells of cigarettes
the swallow tattoo tastes of salt and brine,
                   Shoulder blade/teeth/sharp/minor/key change

This is the proof we needed to know that the woman who loves too hard
/much/often.
[The single task of waiting has now become an act of violent disrespect towards oneself.]
She is not a little girl who was simply unwrapped into grown up clothes.
She is brass and fingerprints and all things haunting
and I am her -- the wailing alto,
asking the streets if they have your forwarding address.

This song was intended for you,
In case you didn't know.

& even the damp reed can splinter.

Summerland
Kevin Morris

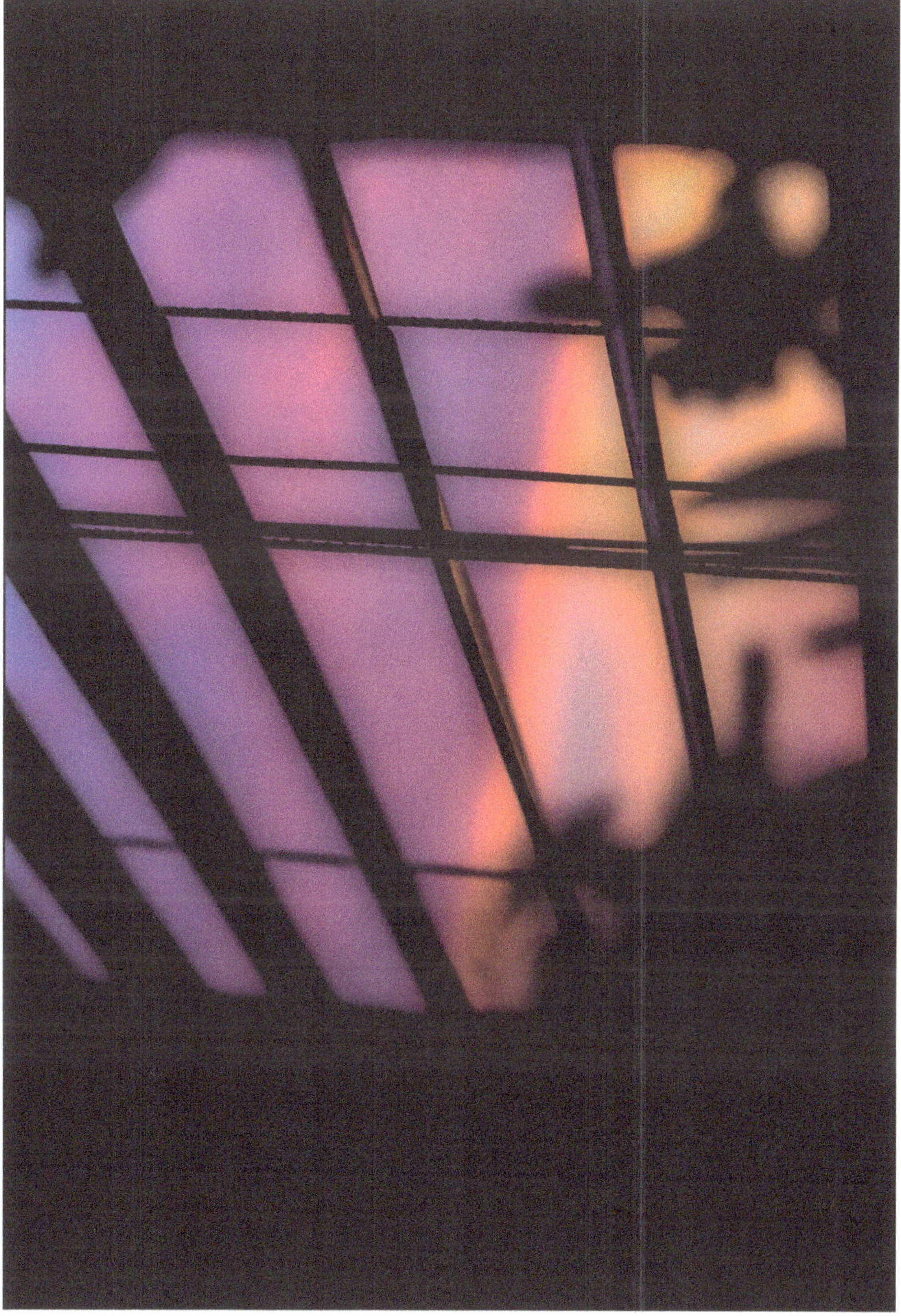

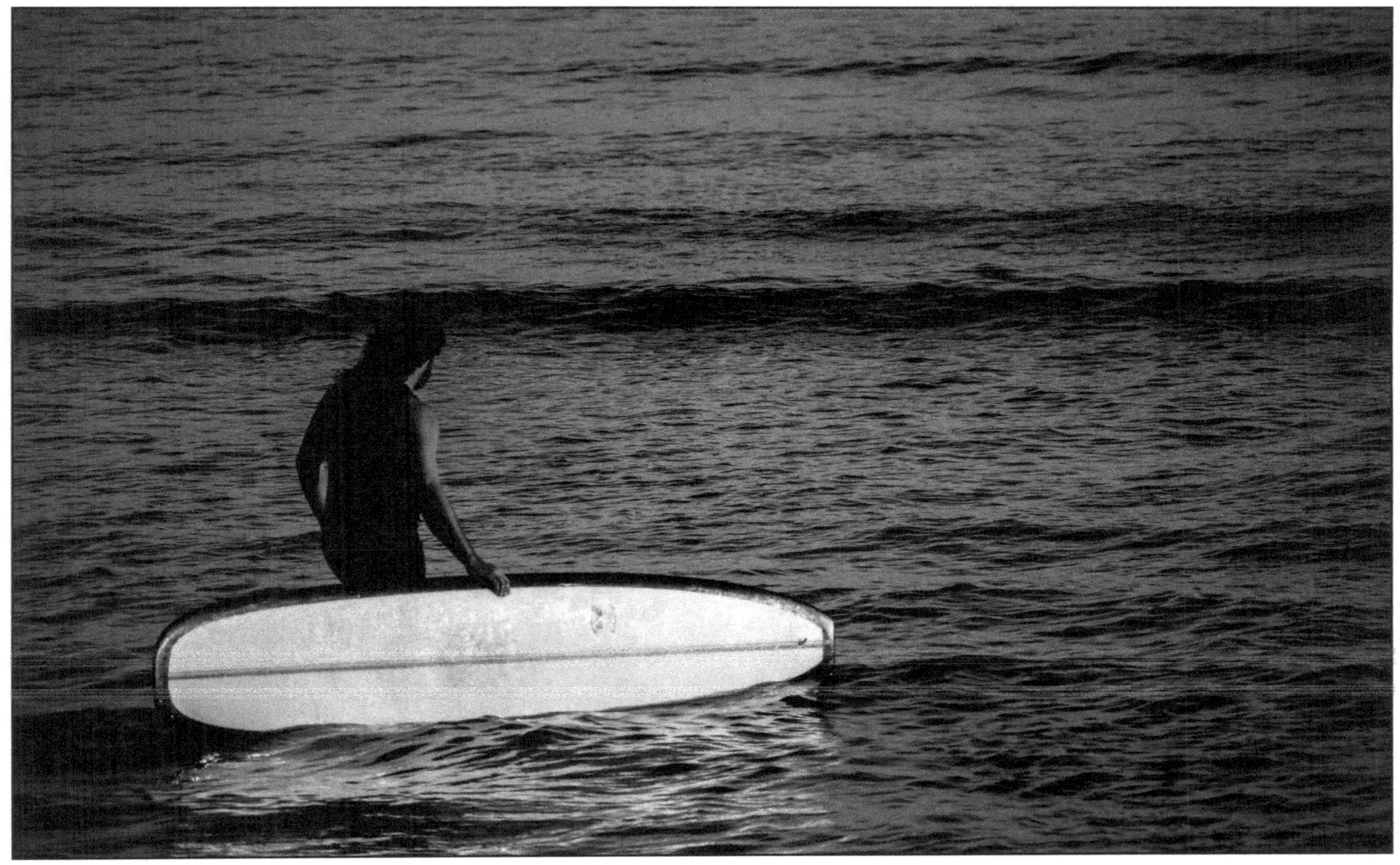

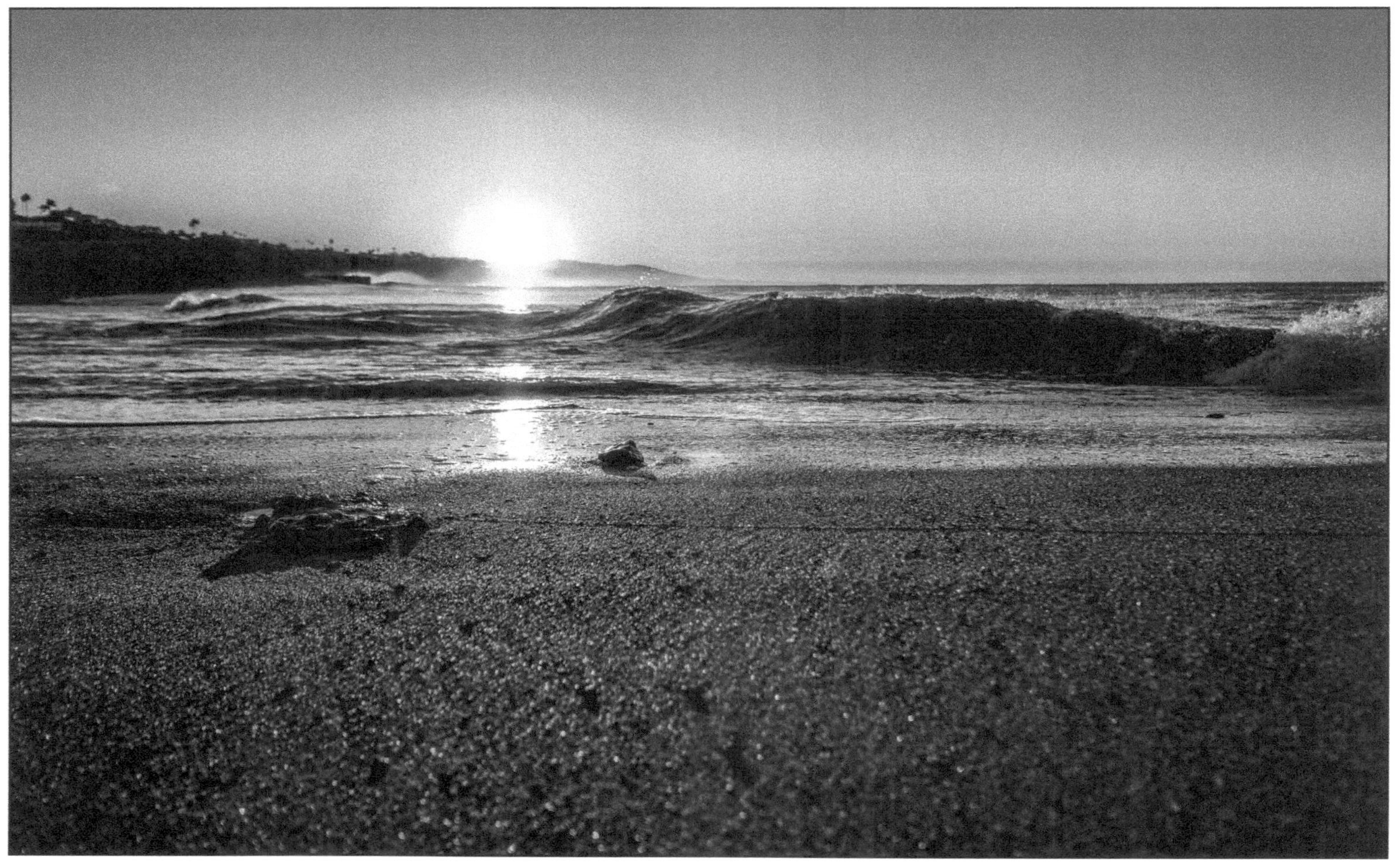

13

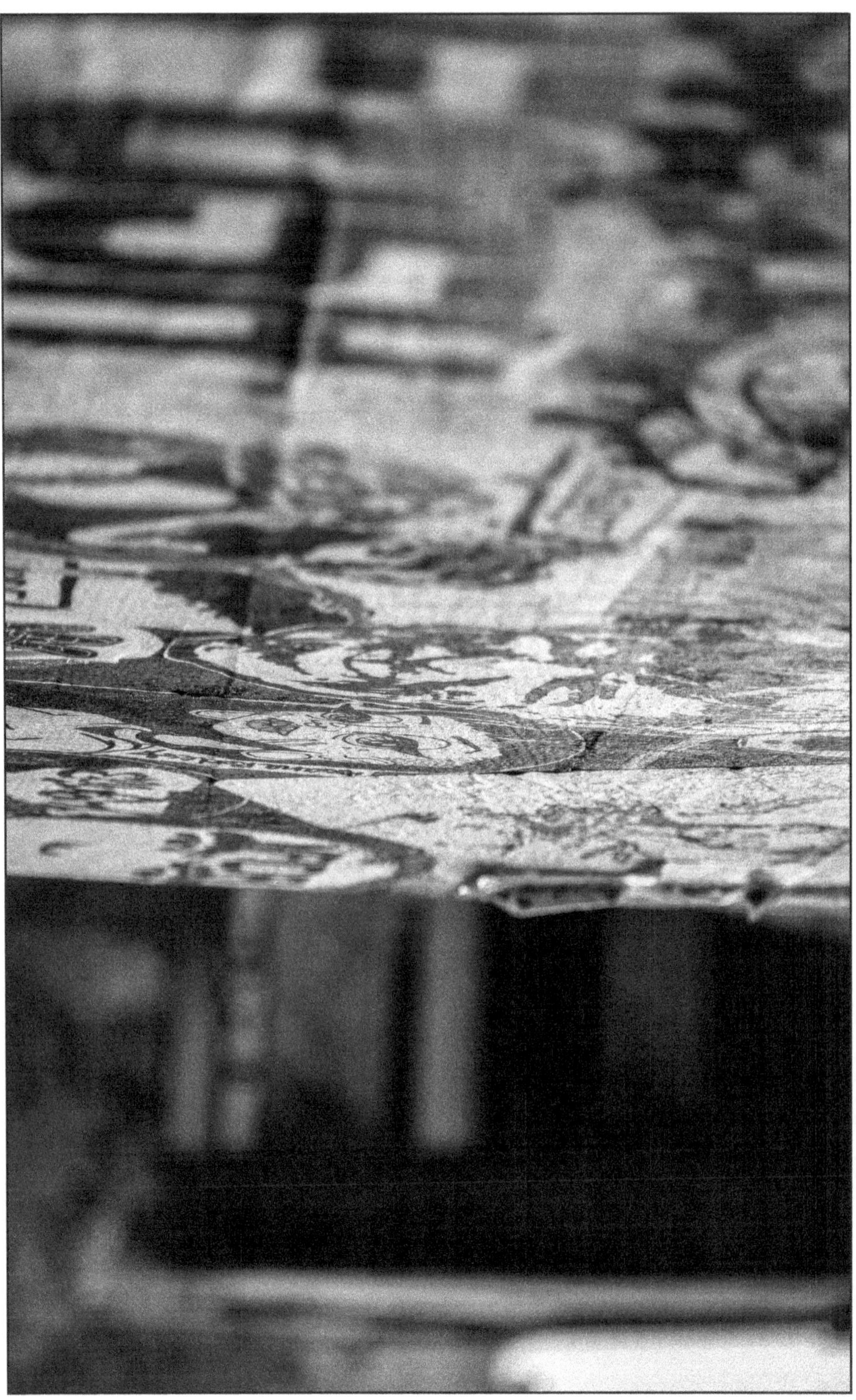

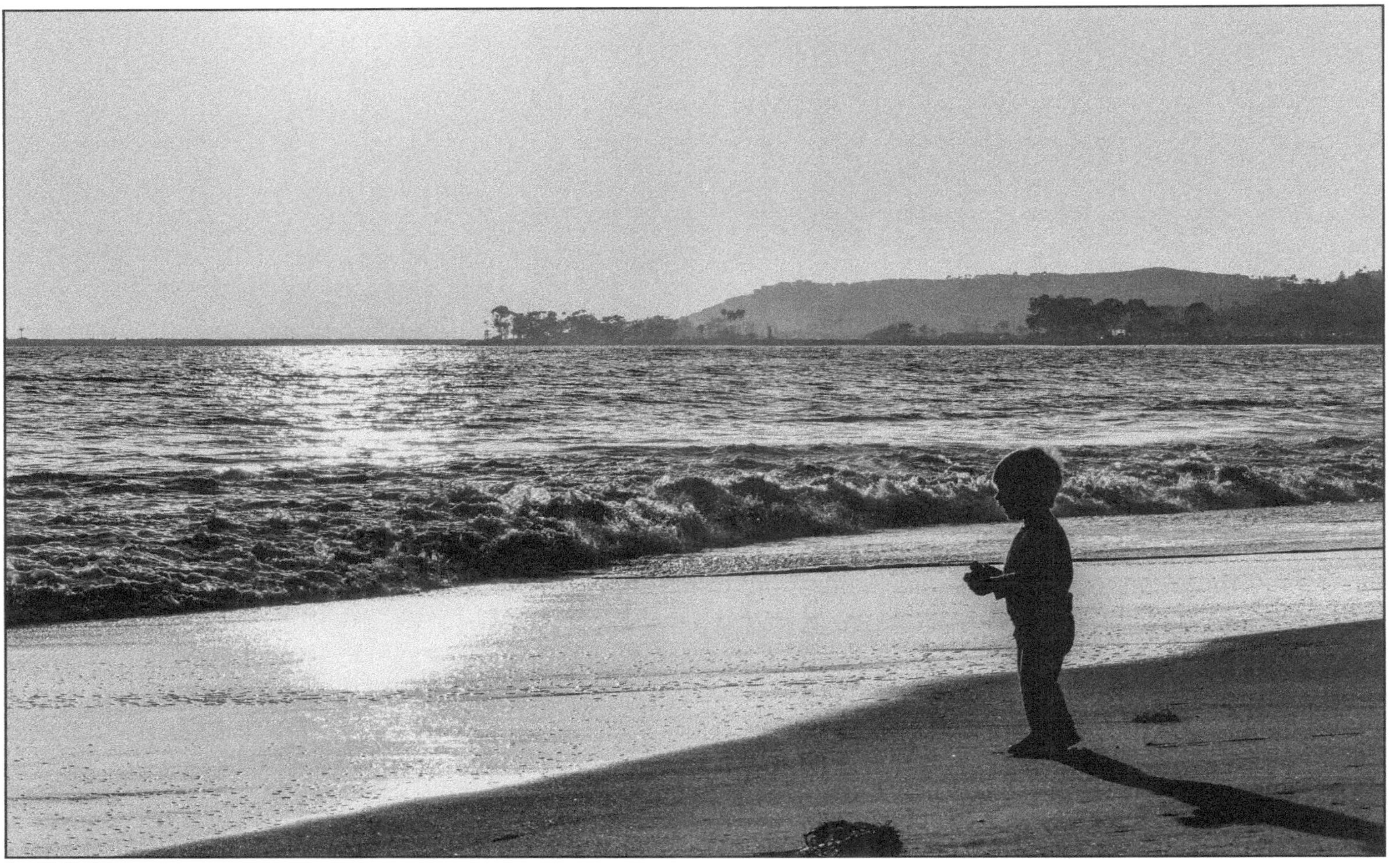

Pink Velvet, Tight Ribbon

Wisteria Deng

Beneath the quiet waves hide sea creatures and strange
monsters. Coming to life before the first stroke
on a blank canvas, between two pale fingers.
I spill myself over your
sharp edges. I am
thick drops dripping from your frame. And you rise
from sea creatures and young monsters.
Naked.
A stream of primal desire sucked
to a small studio. A sack of lava swirled inside
a stuffed rabbit. Pencil in your hand, each gesture a siren calling
for the indecisive winter.

I am thick drops dripping
from your frame and you are in mine.
A few more innocent gazes and a groaning mouth to contain
your thorn. A frame expands. Stranded.
Strip. Spread wide
to fit you. A frame
with pink velvet tied as a ribbon, tight
as an invitation.

You are static electricity. You command
strange sea creatures
and young monsters with prodding thorn.
Gather around me. Streams
of secret wishes and safe words.
Flood me.
With brute force and specks of dust,
flood me.
Pink velvet, born to desire, its curvature
fits the spine of sea creatures.
Tie a ribbon around my waist, tighten
your strained caress.
Make me a gift
of half-filled ocean, swirling
poison. Make me streams
of your primal sketch and I will flood you
with the same search. Come
to my cave. There we grow strange sea
monsters
together. Watch them
probe thorns into each other's mouth.

Tie pink velvet around their open legs. Make them
bend. Two limbs would make a ribbon. Two would beg
for a feast.

Love Letter

Niku Rice

I have starved you of my admiration
For far too long, marred you with blind curses
And forgotten your sweetness, your valleys
And creeks marked by worry and dull sorrow,
Lost track of the miles traveled, the hands held,
The sunsets swallowed whole or in brush strokes.

But I awoke this morning ready to
Love you completely, caress each callous
And blemish with songs of adoration
As for the variation in each stone
Tumbling through rough streams for ages on end,
Never wishing to be anything else.

This beautifully deflated body
Has ebbed and flowed with rich golden milk,
Sustained the life of three radiant lights,
Built an empire of desire and hunger,
Bound only by the decorum of norms
And the shame of loving these tired bones.

The space between what was and what will be
stretched thin and translucent, like a secret
whispered in the dark. Rings in my trunk mark
time with echoes reverberating
between the orbits of "was" and "will be",
A constantly shifting song of patience.

I love you, with buzzing curiosity
Over your ever changing landscapes.
I love you, round temple of pleasure,
My stupa etched with the history of me.
I love you, dear body, for holding me
Up to the mirror of this sweet moment.

something different
Emerson DeLaCamara

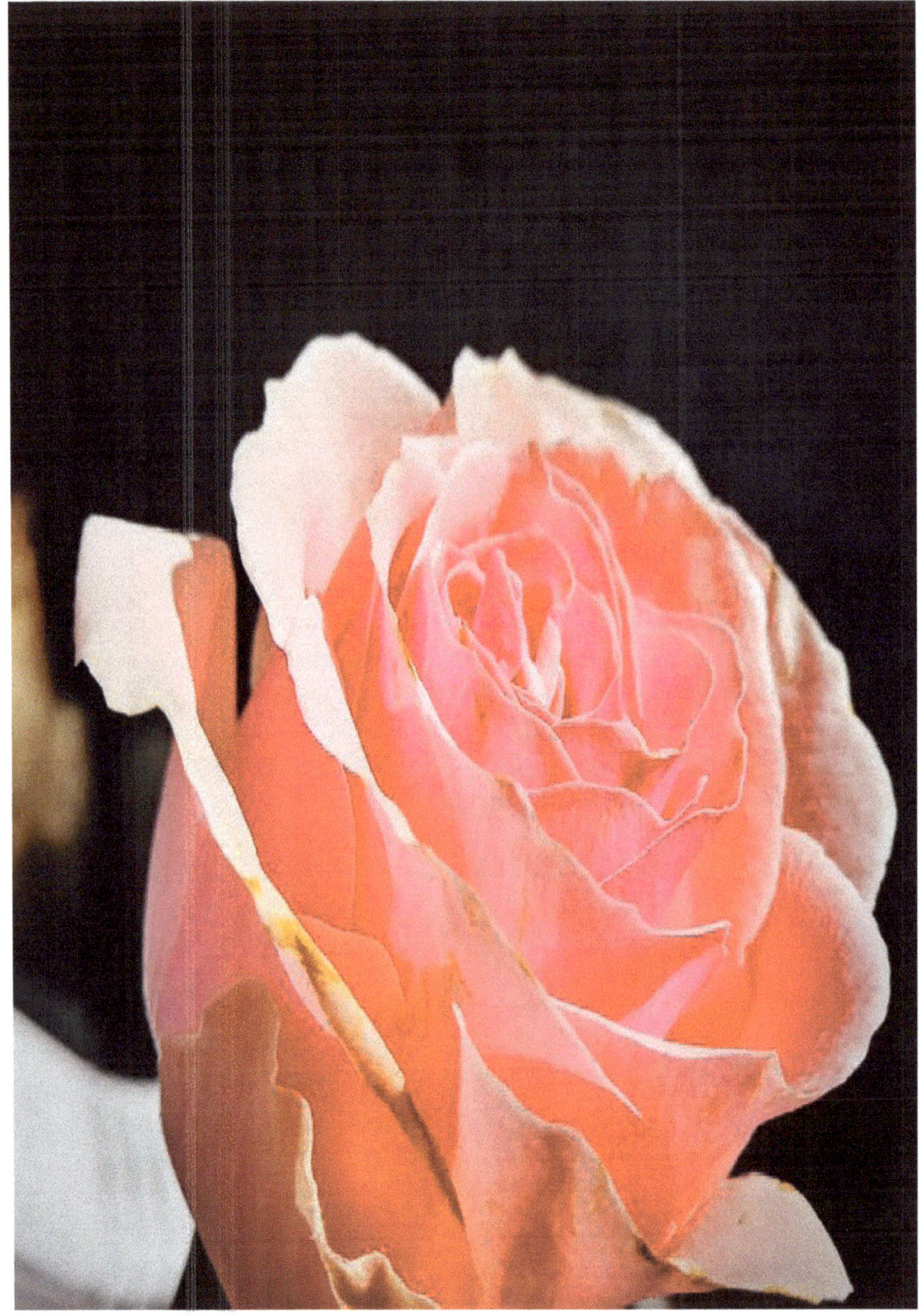

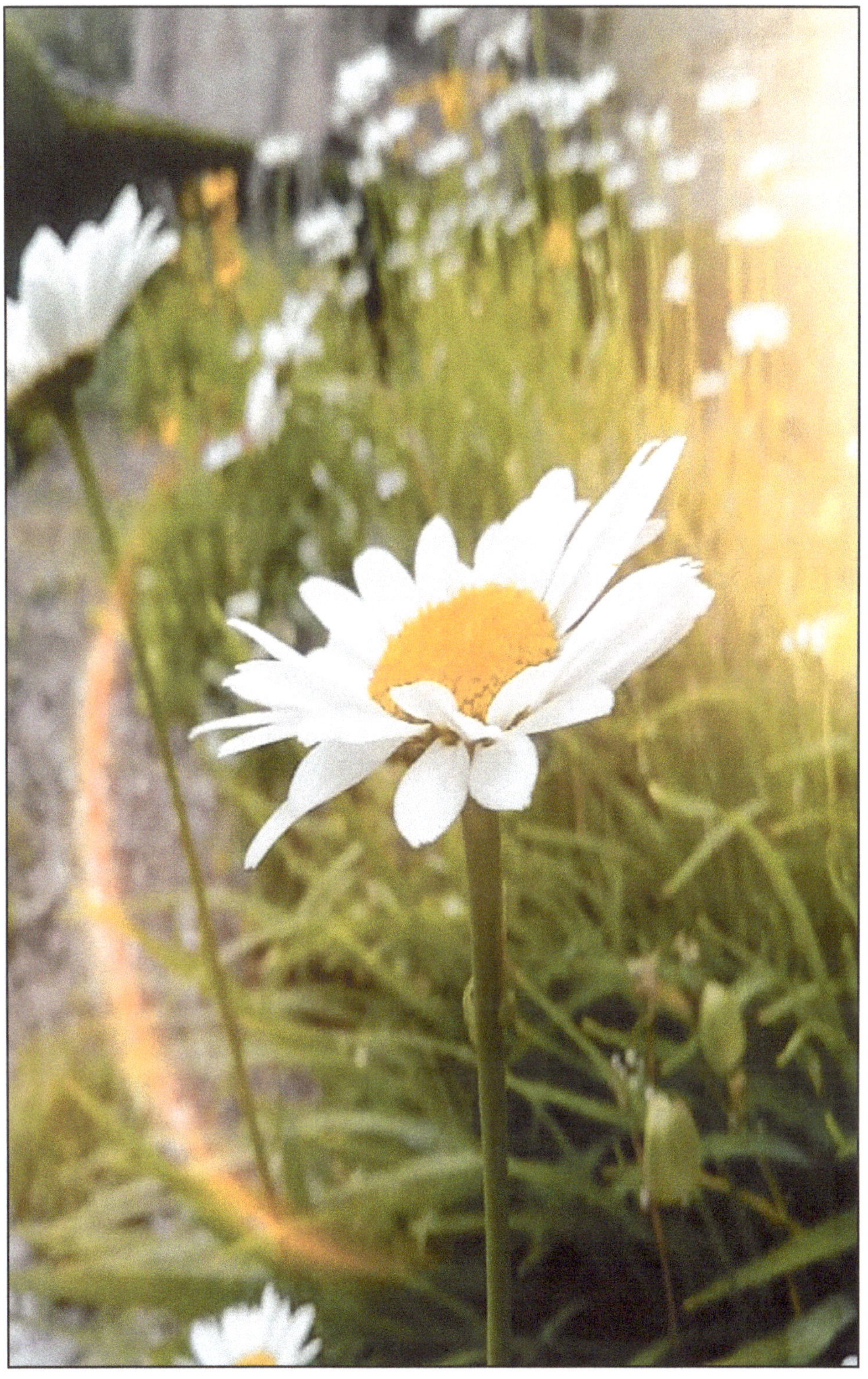

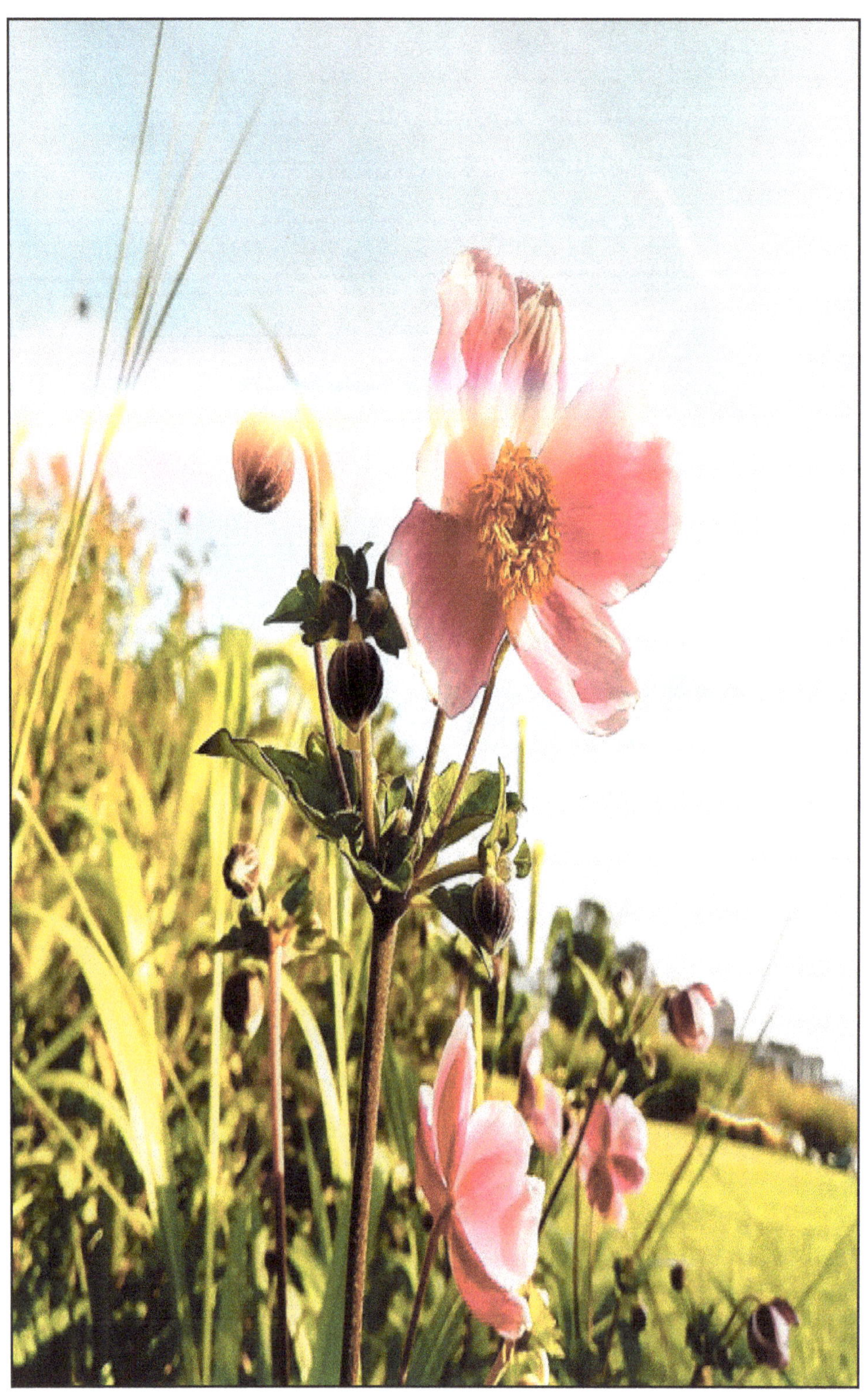

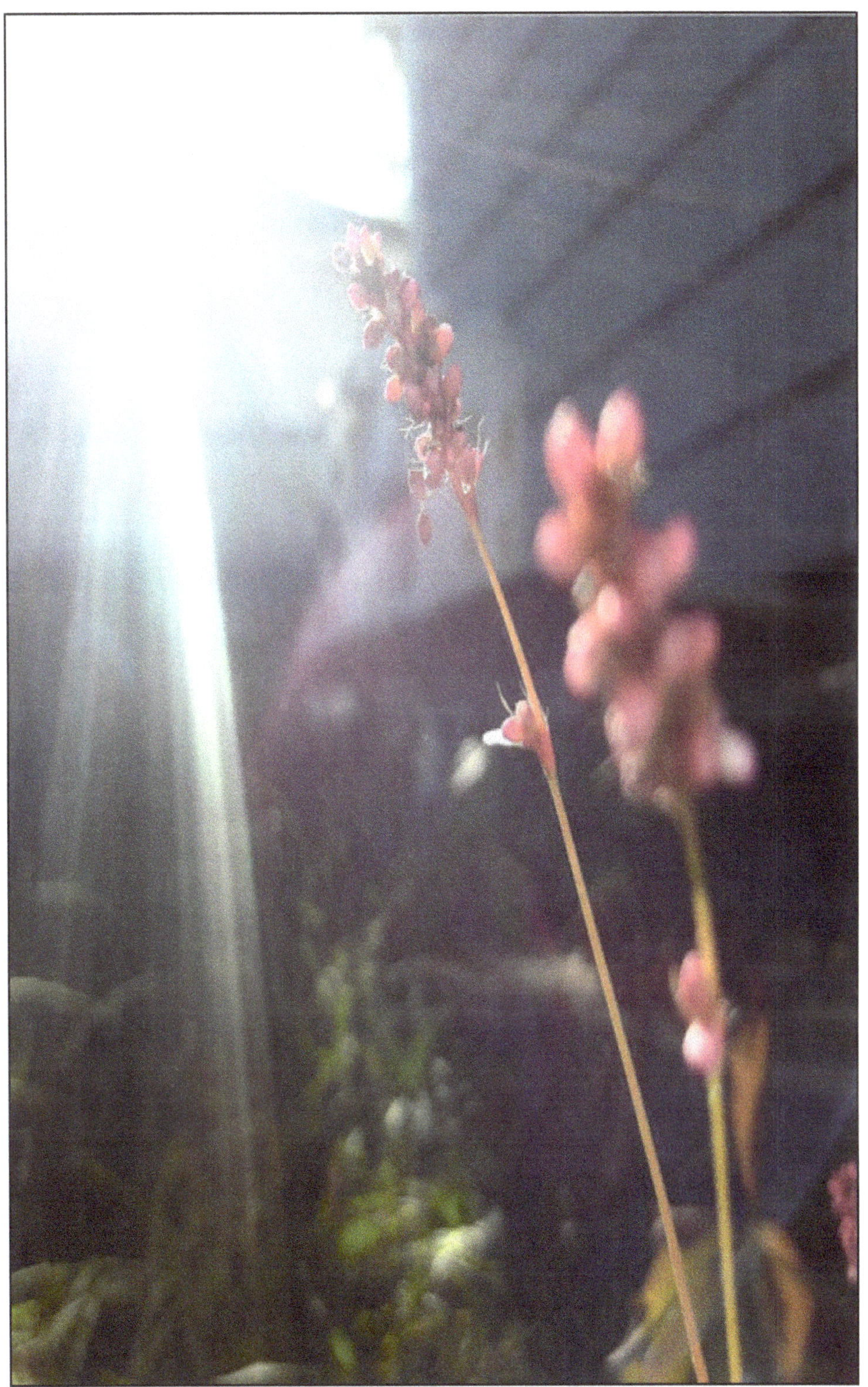

heart of a fish

Lizz Ehrenpreis

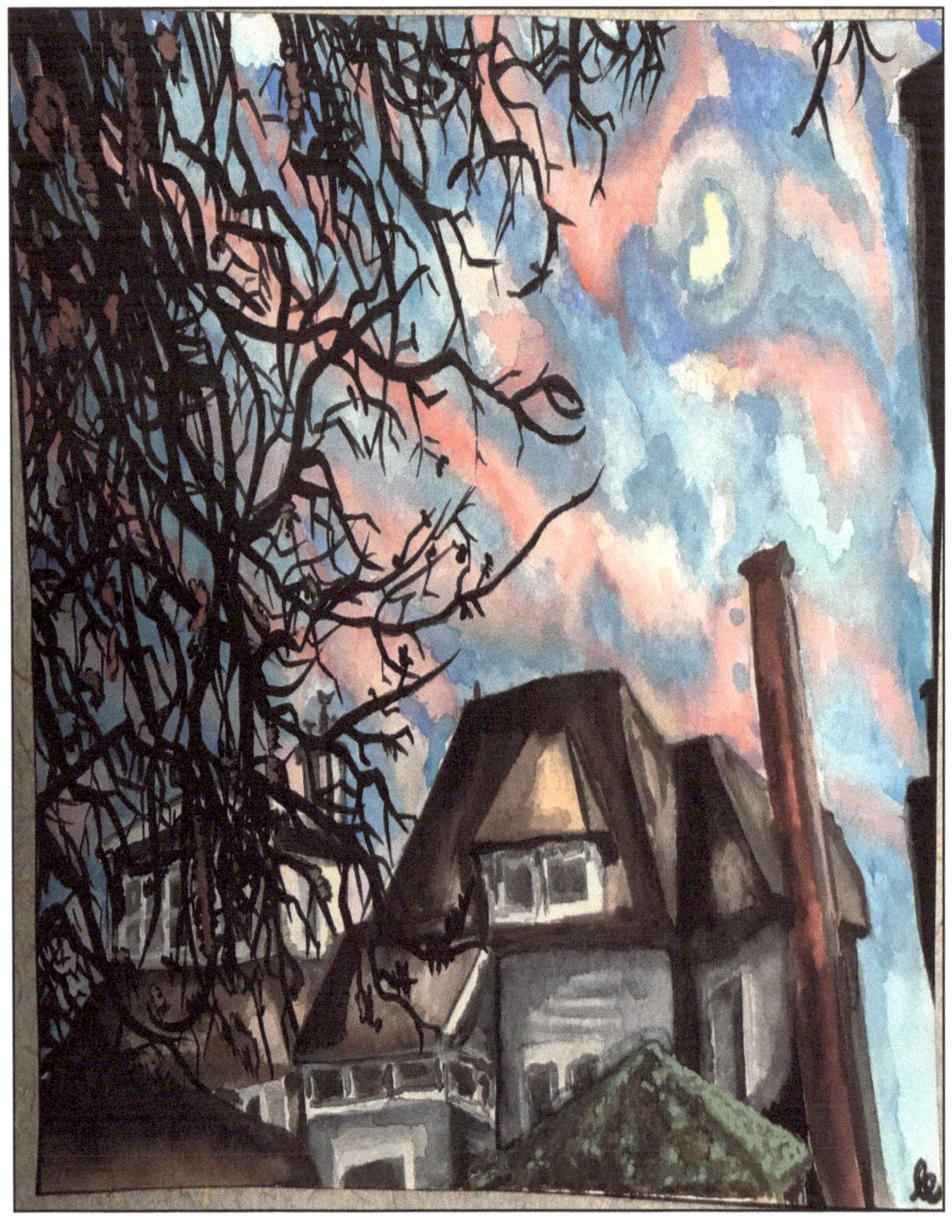

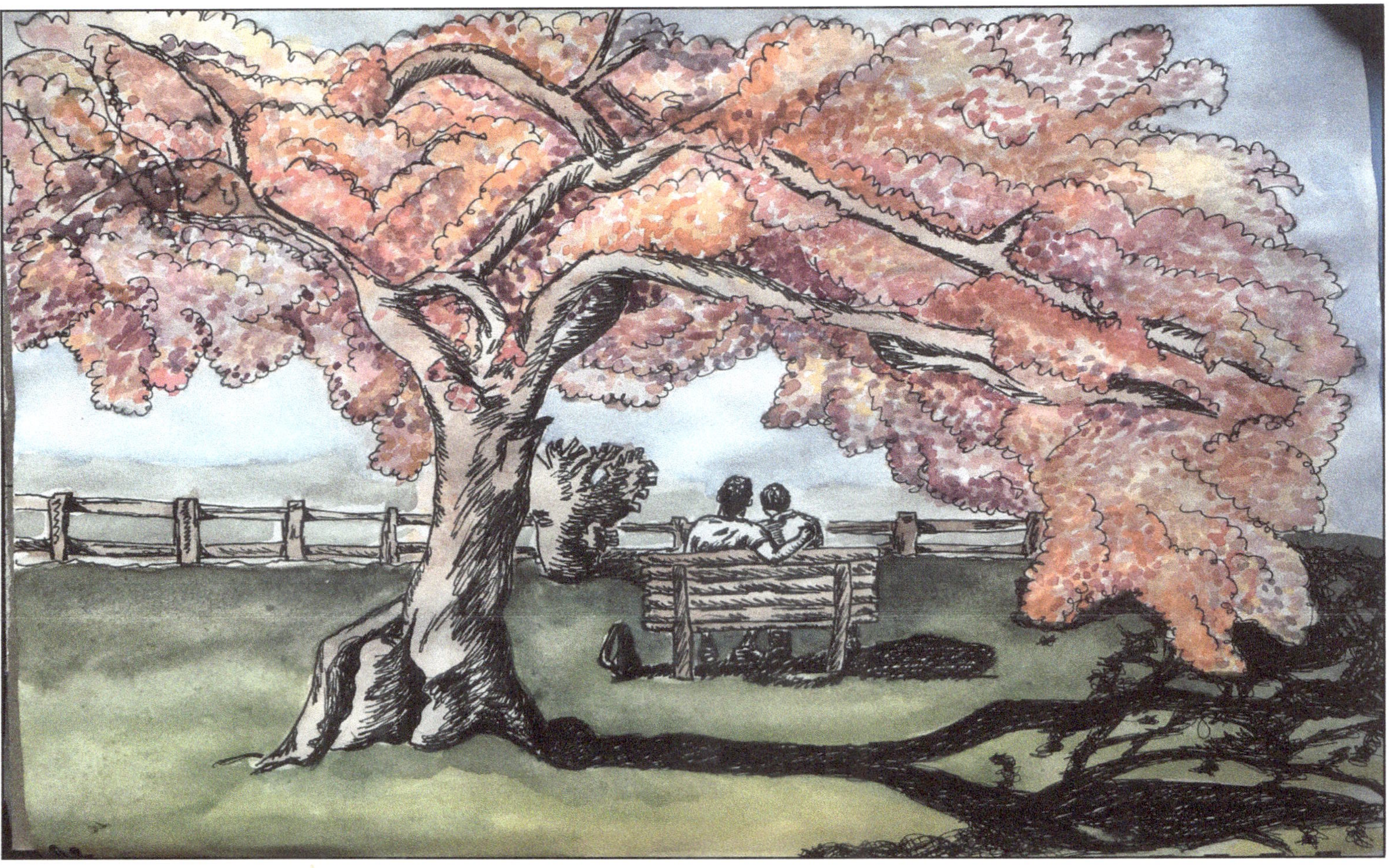

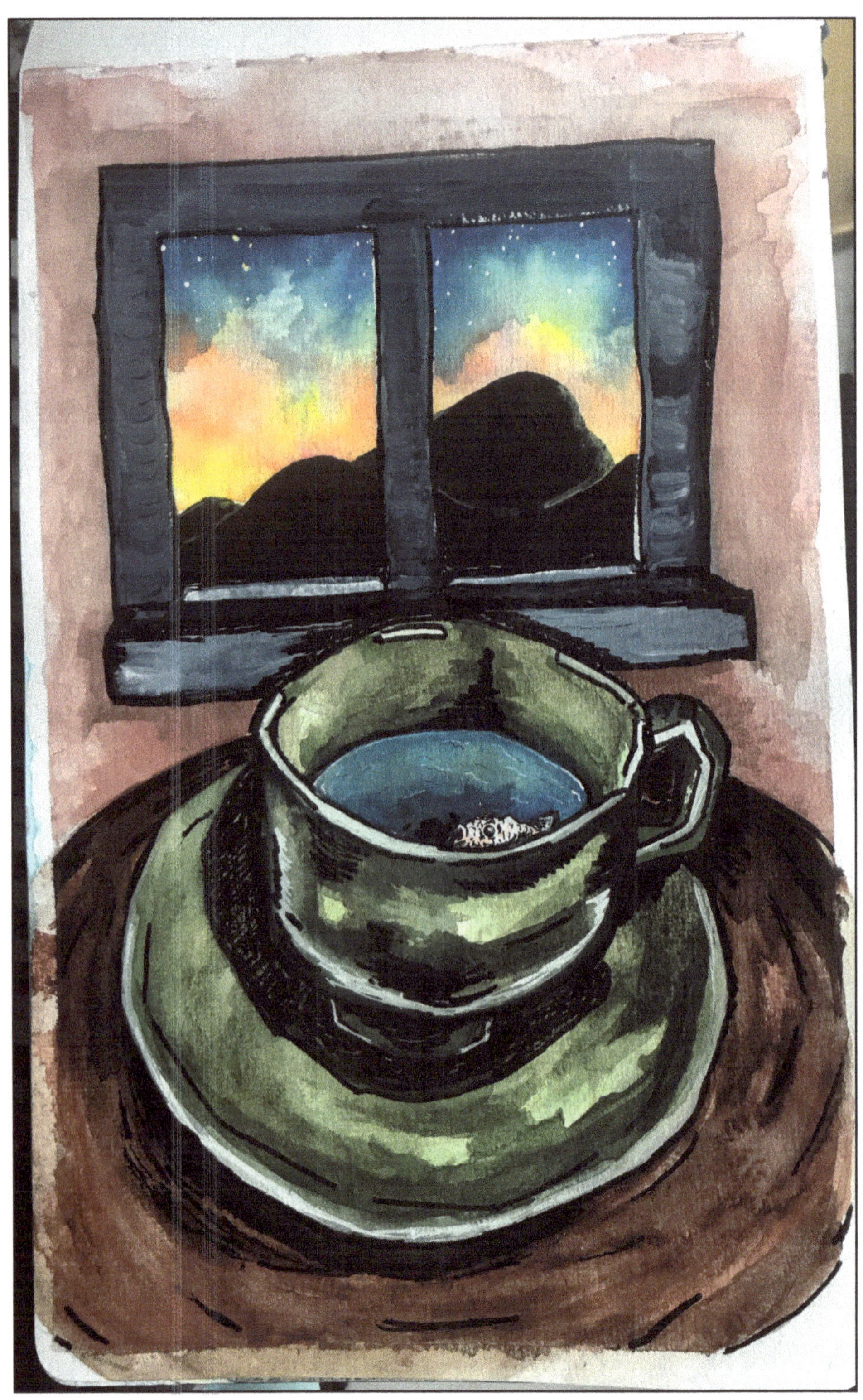

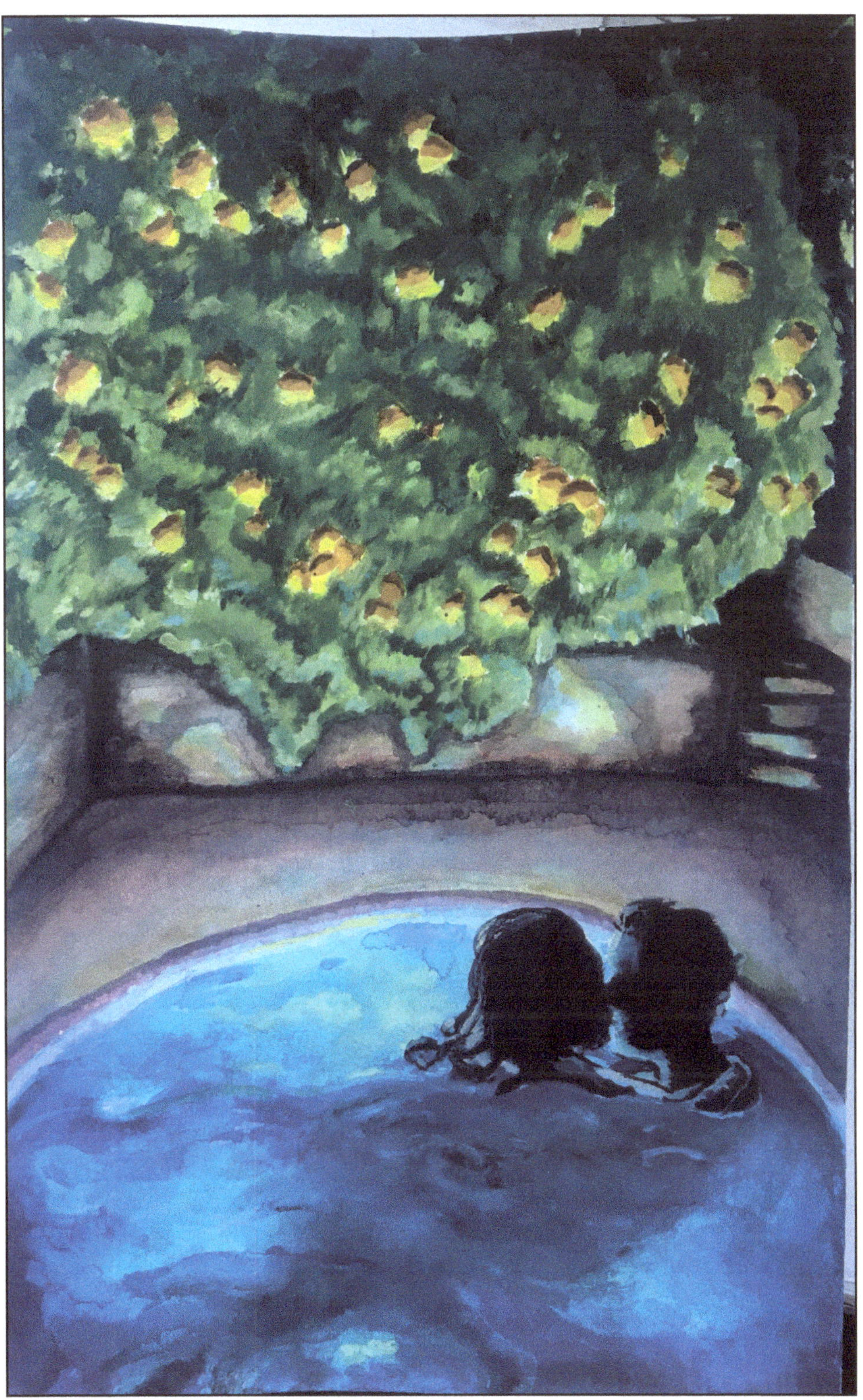

Anatomy of a Carrot

A. Pikovsky

open
move these brittle legs
spread them
"over & out" like shea butter
across the flushed flesh of carrot meat
enter this garden
then feast on
(*reciprocity*)

open
kiss these tender knees
unpeel them
drip for me like hot beeswax
coat the yolk bound to my bony shell
i am wrinkled & lapped by your papery husk
unseal me for
(*protection*)

Open
with these hungry hips
pull from their bulbs like sun-colored taproot
hold them, then blow
[Enter: Ram's Horn Ritual]
beneath the supple soil another voyeur vegetates
make a circle of salt, dressed in seeds & musk
from tongue to mouth, then fold to flap, begins the harvest of
(*lust*)

Jodie Filan Art

Jodie Filan

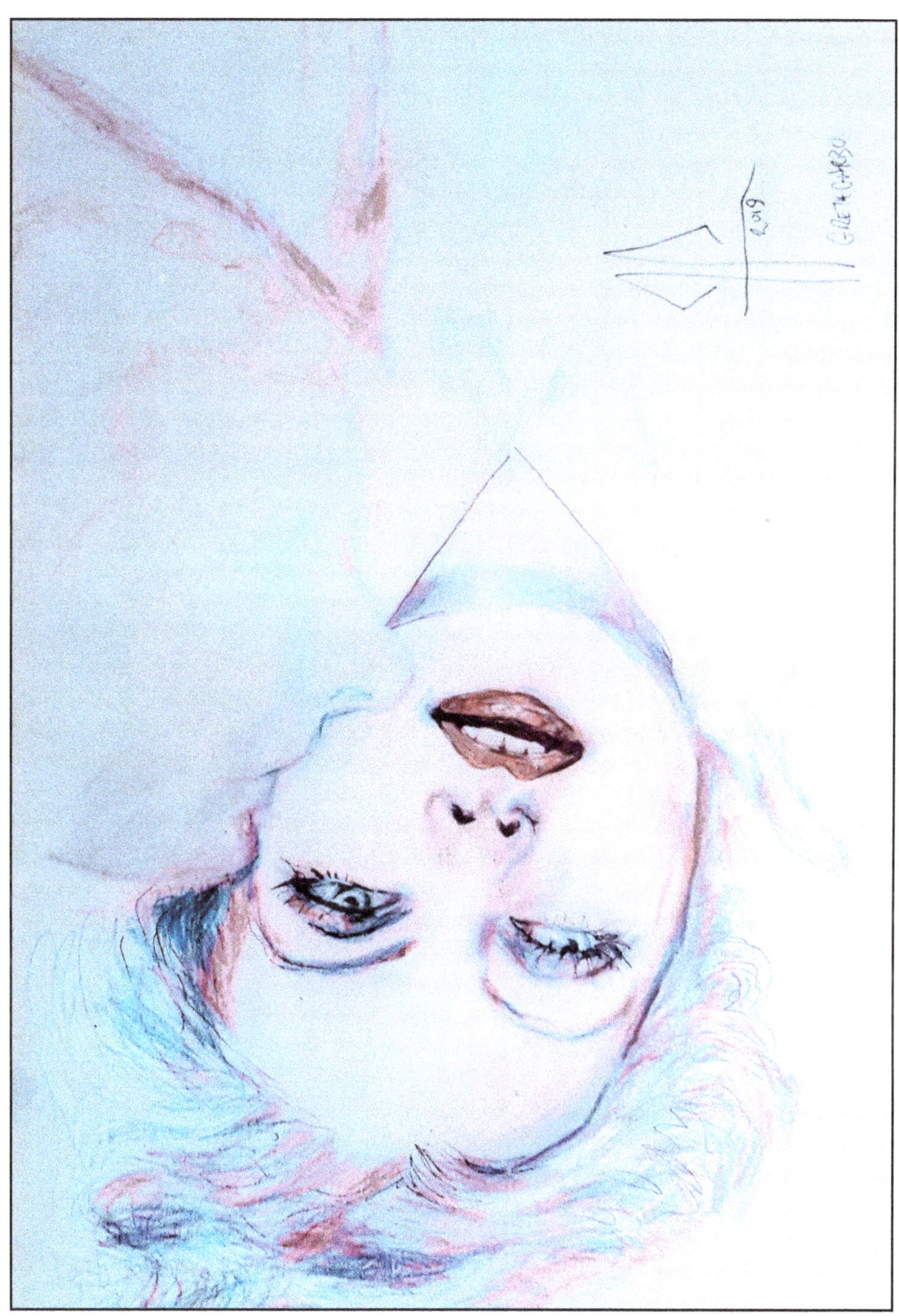

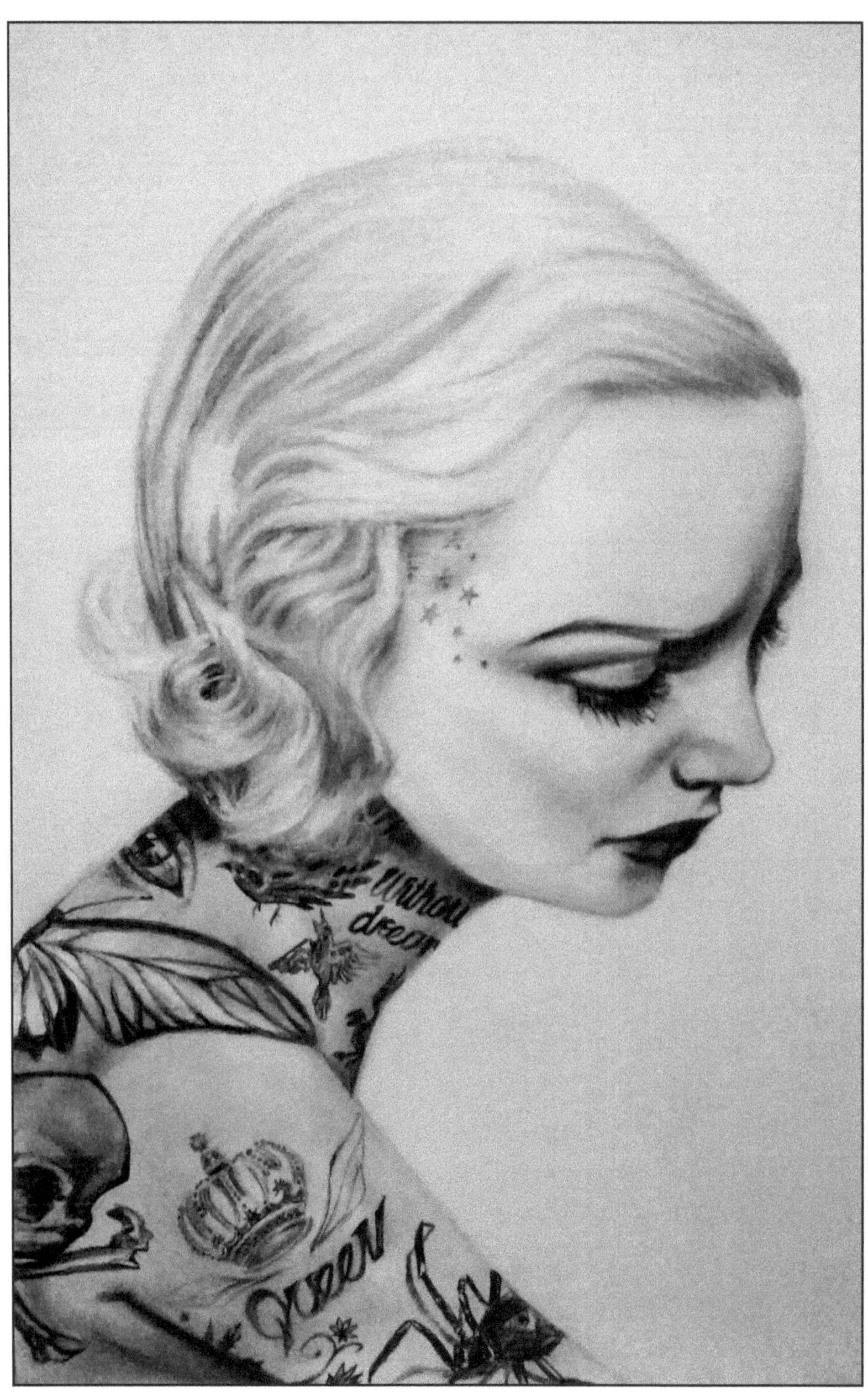
without
dream
Queen

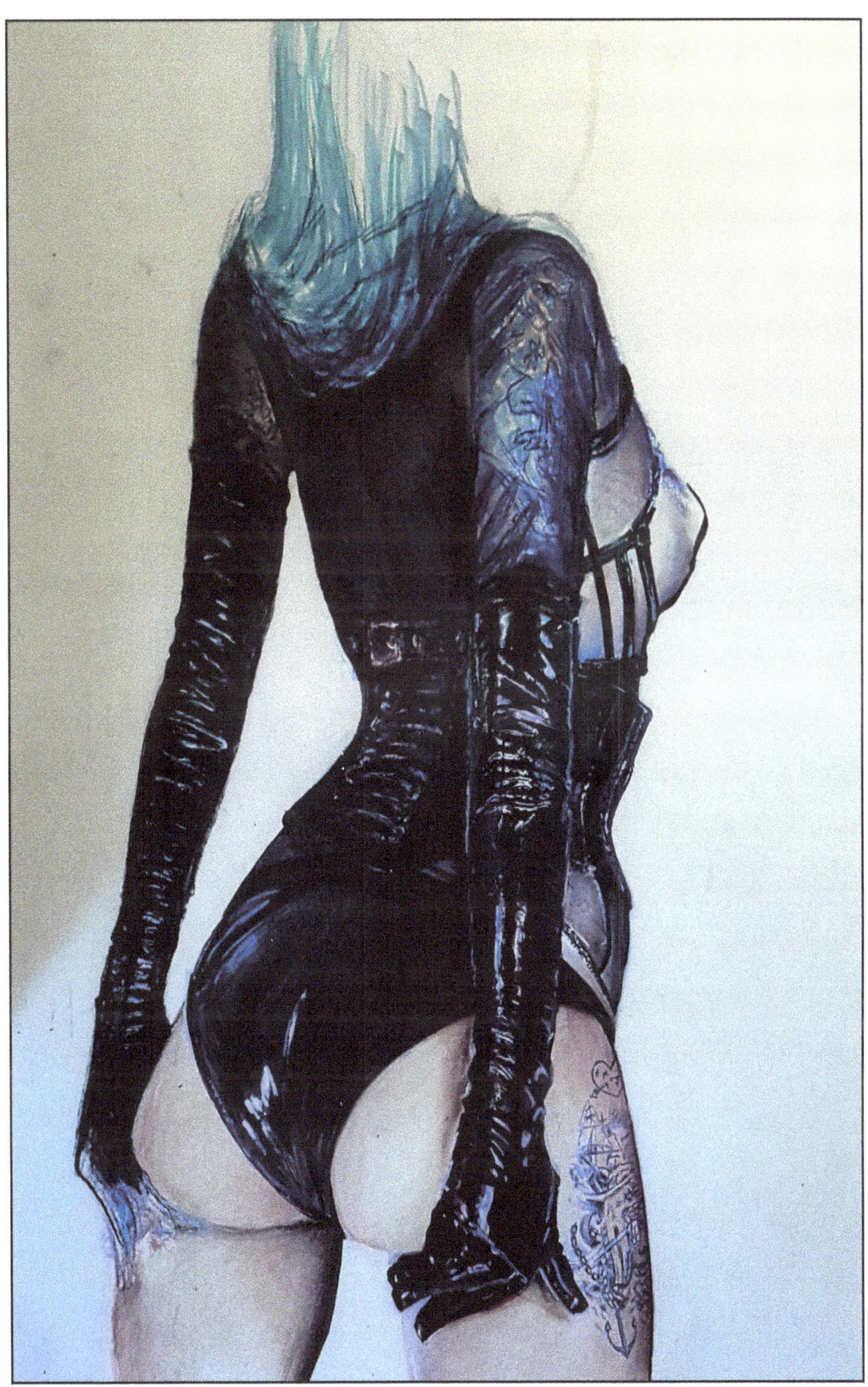

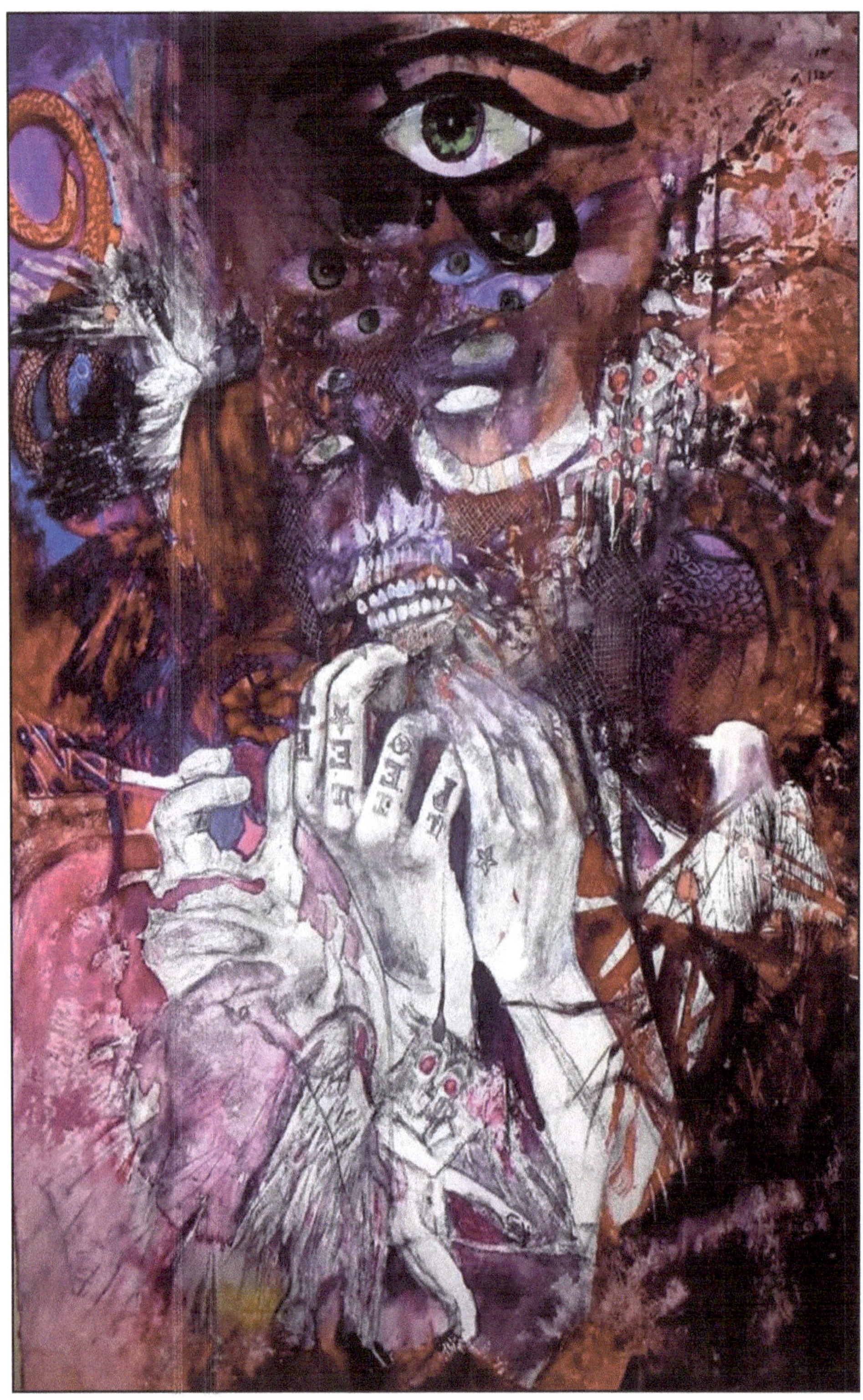

defamation

Brenna Lakeson

The words sat in my voice box,
for years,
my lips couldn't make the words.
When I tried to say them,
my voice turned to vapor
and poured out of my mouth like smoke,
evaporating.
Hearing my mouth spit out the syllables
made it true,
and the longer it stayed trapped under my tongue
the longer I could try to erase it.

Memories are sometimes a relief
but the one with your taste in my mouth
is a drilling into my eardrum.
With a small hope
of releasing the pressure
I stick my hands down my throat
and force the words up and out.
They are messy but they are true.
I don't know quite how to arrange them.

Me,
                        too.

Still, you find me.
You are ravenous
and tear at the flesh of my words
like a wolf on the hunt.
You tell me that my words
are a house of straw,
and that you plan to set it on fire
if I don't do it first.
My story will go up in smoke,
you warn.

Instead,
I fortify them
in the fire
into steel.

Havishammed +1

Laura Lee

She used crutch
as weapon.
Here and here and here, see this?

Boxes filled, new home needs
but no new home for that
bastard of a man left her
not at the altar but
in the recovery room.

Boxes now used as ashtrays
boxes now used as homes for
black cat, calico cat
cat with one eye,
ammonia smell keeping out
all but the havishammed.

One box for the black dog
panting in the heat
but still waking Havishammed +1
when she fell asleep with red glow
that dog, with so little place to move
between, among those boxes
turned in a circle, barking snapping
whining, peeing for a life
woke her before fire
before *Damn.*

THAÏS
Tia Harestad

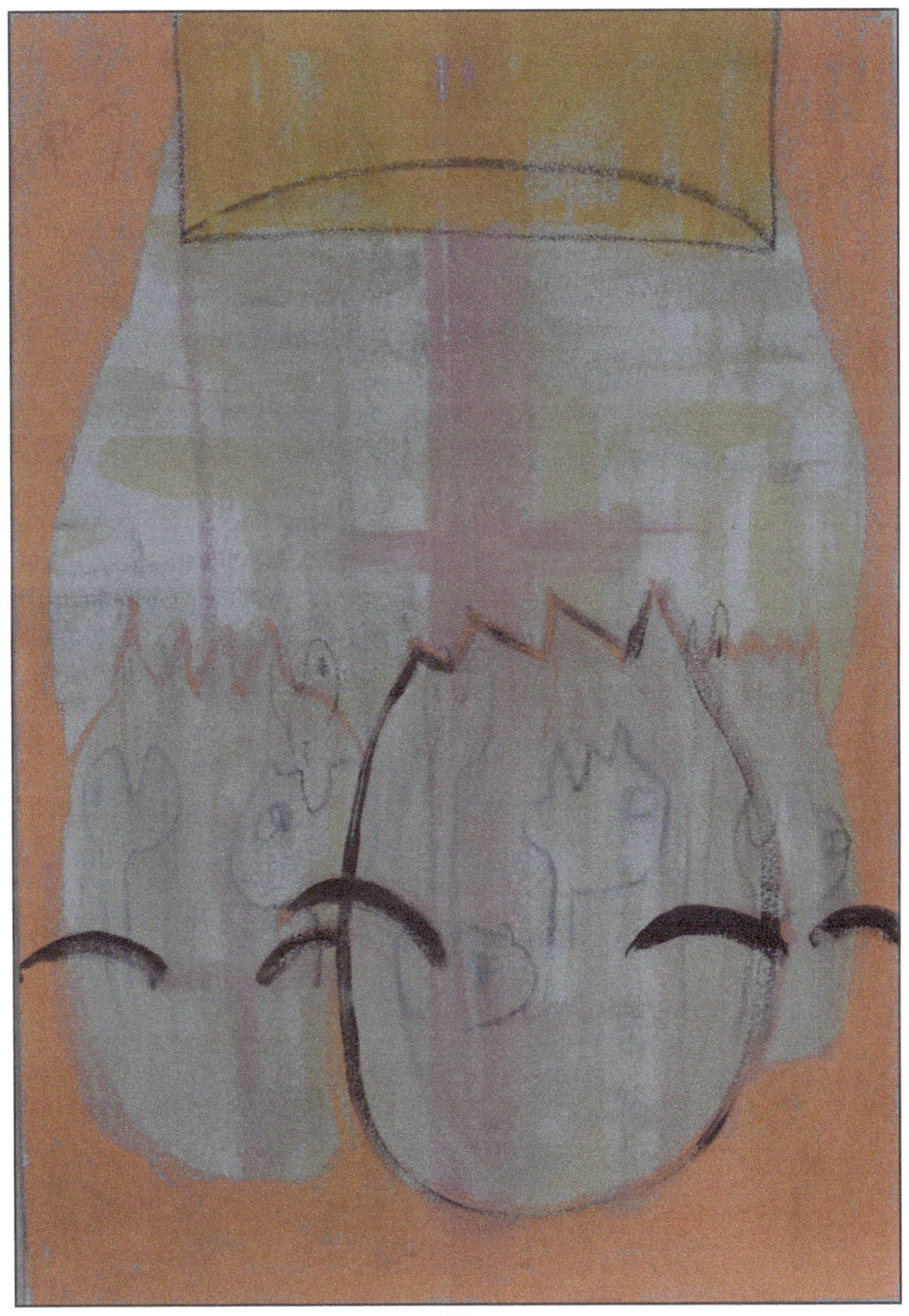

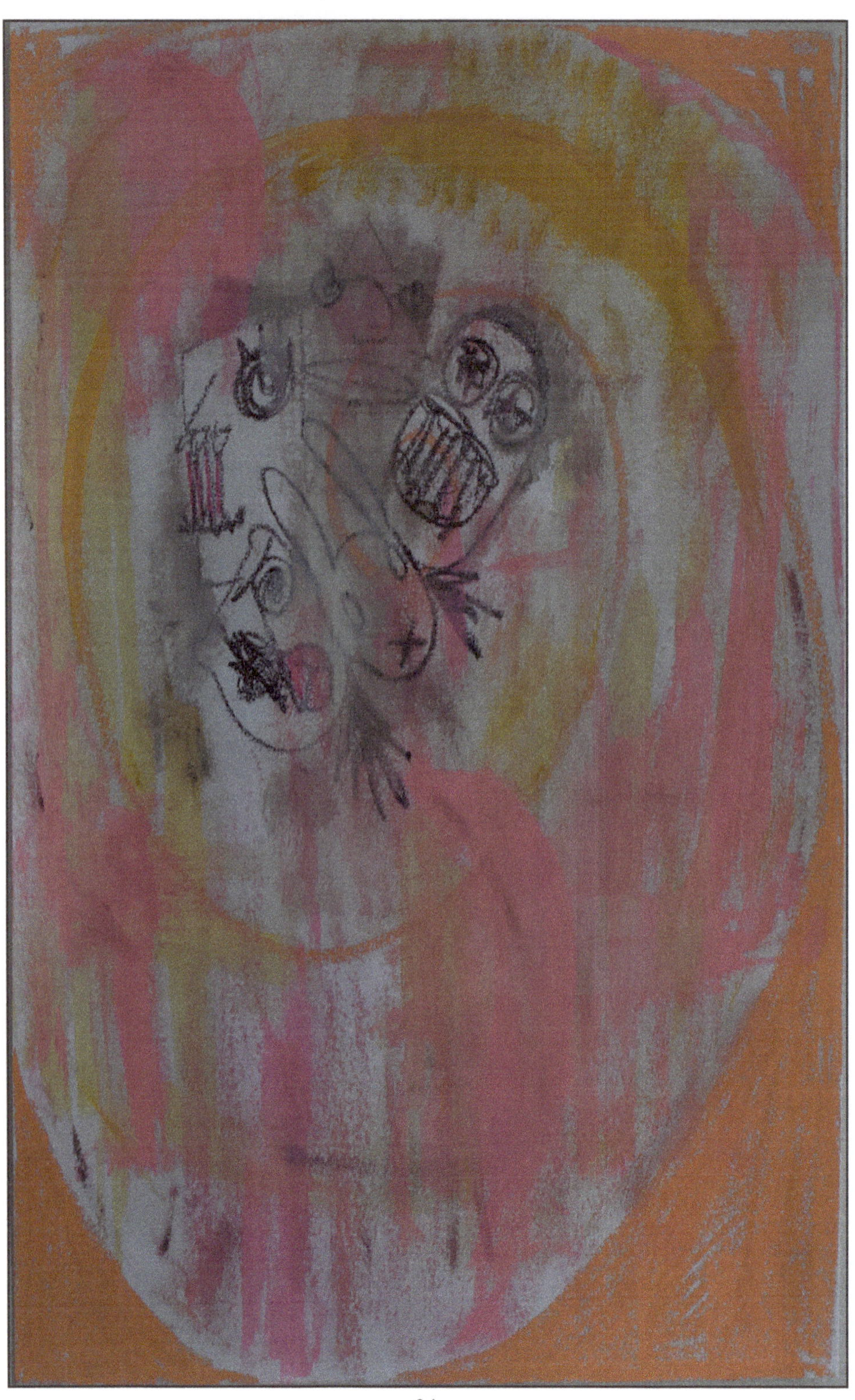

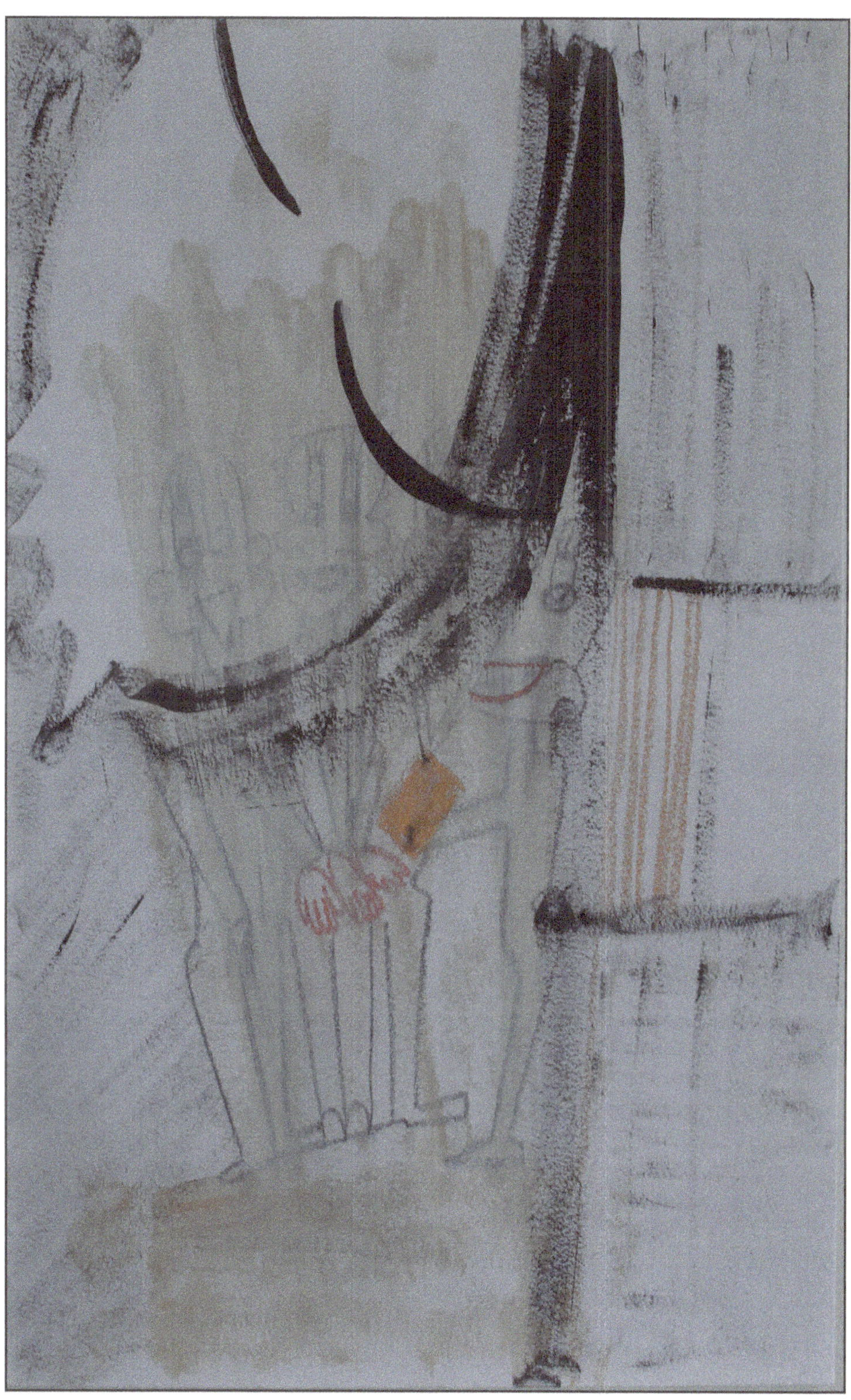

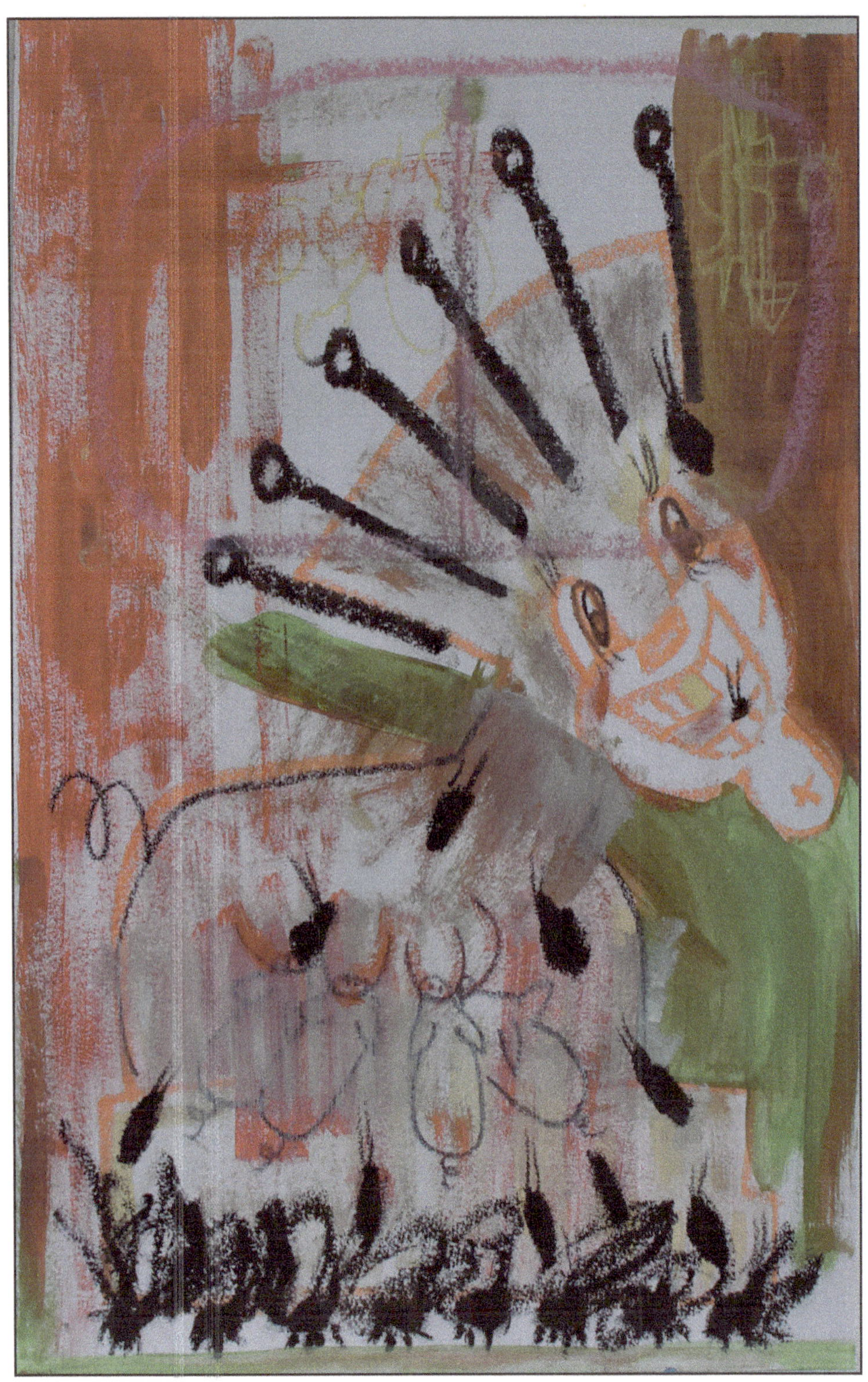

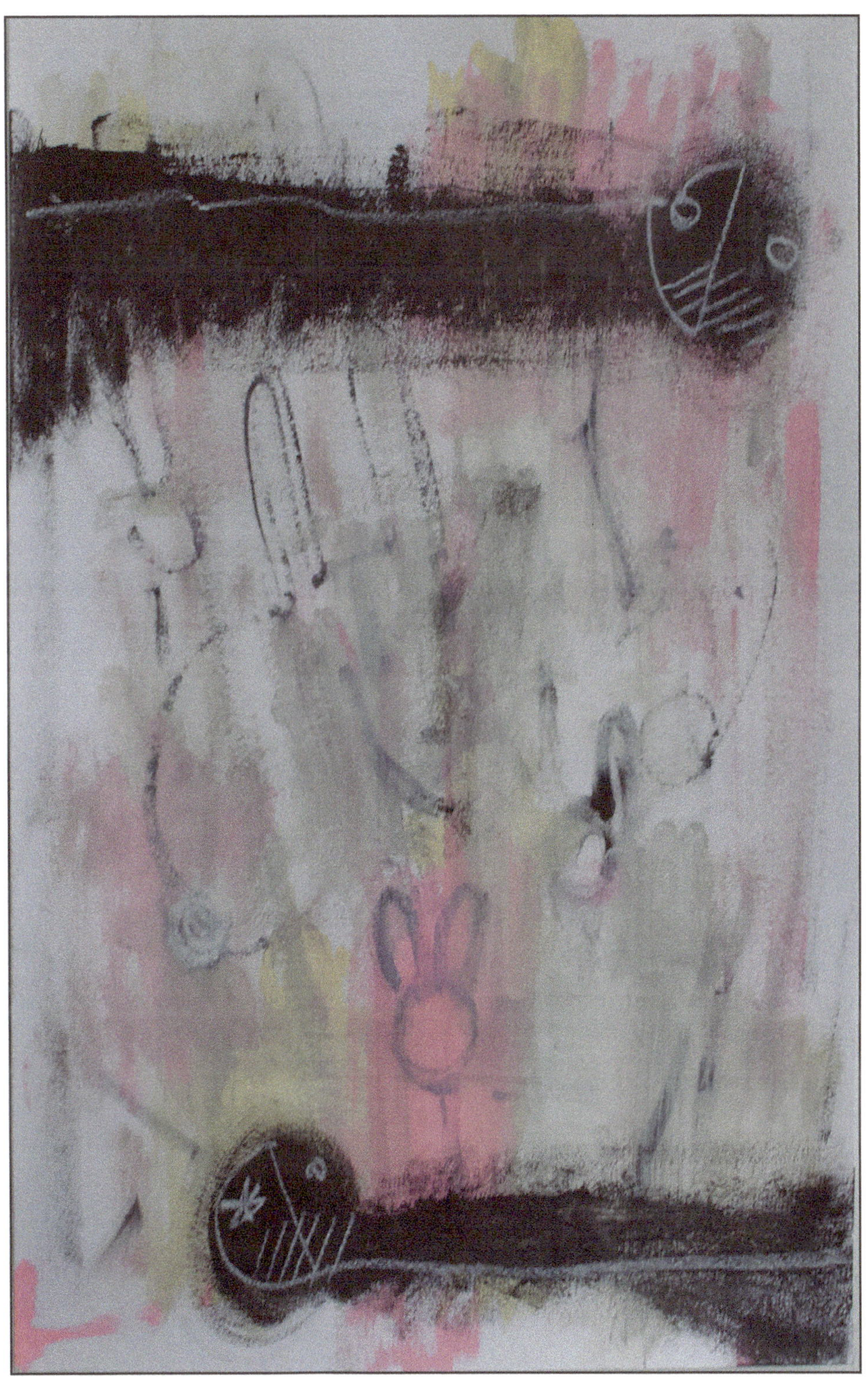

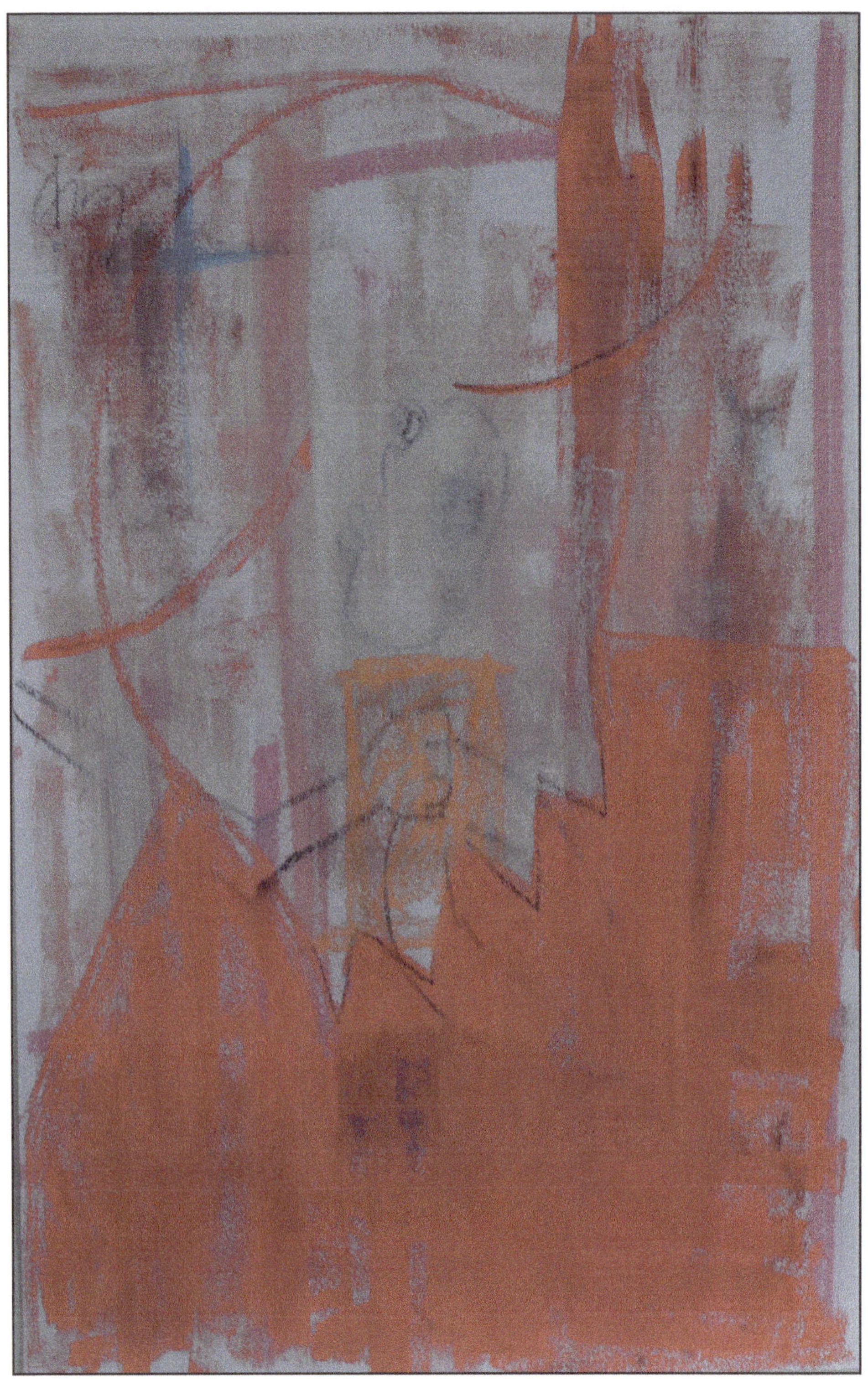

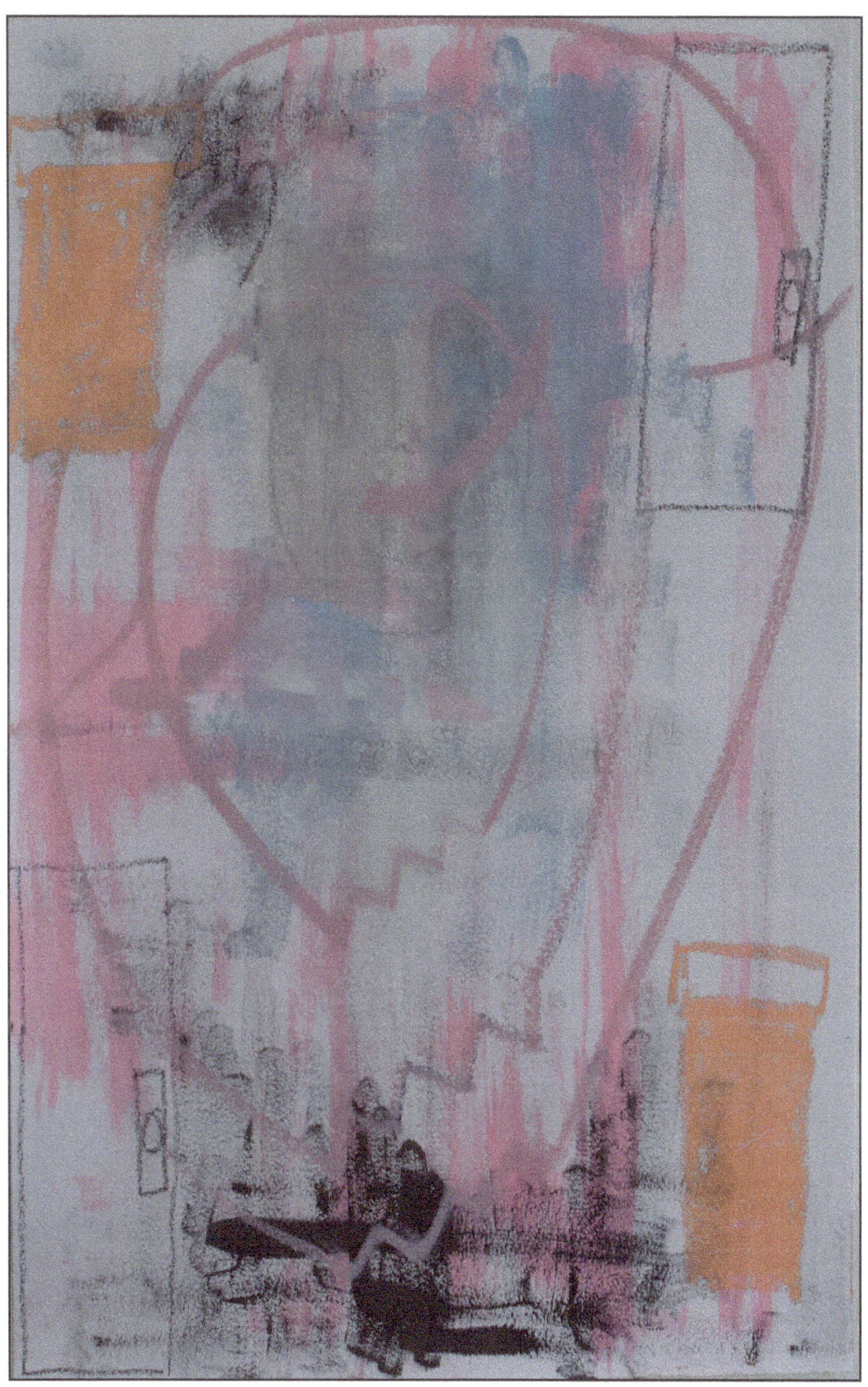

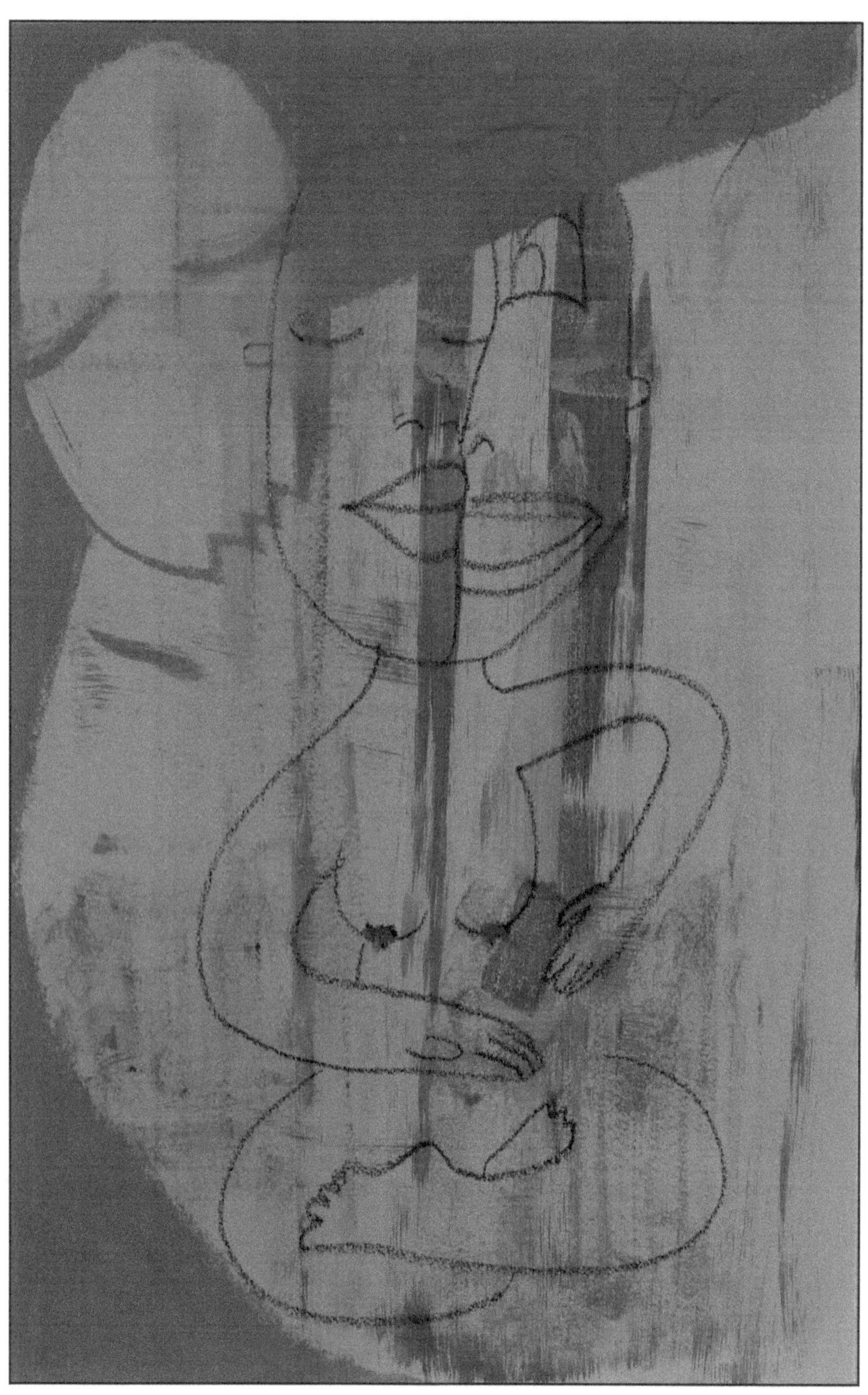

The House Fell

Josie Turner

It was like an earthquake. That shaking begins, crashing noise you don't hear
coming from anywhere, shaking rattles, continues,
     until you cannot think anymore. It is that kind of shaking
I hear and feel when I see a motorcyclist on a rainy day.
I remember the artist, Michael Fajans, and it is that kind of shaking
I think about when you leave in the morning, and I know
I have not a rational reason to worry but I do worry, will you come home?
It does not make sense, but it is what I think about.
I think about the person who at Michael's funeral described
     how there was blood coming out of his mouth,
I wondered if the red was a red he would have liked, like the red on his paintings
     the painting at the airport,
I wish I could be his magician and pull him out of a hat, make him whole again
     like Michael painted the magician and his rabbit.
I did not even know Michael. But Bill, you and your paint,
     he was a painter and your friend.
I put tomatoes into the fish stew pot, they gurgle, bubble and mix around
     cilantro, olive oil, wine. They are my creation, my work of art
     my wanting to feed you, my wanting to feed myself, mother myself.

****

My mother did not allow me to suckle -
mothers in the 1950's found suckling old fashioned
like making cake from scratch. Cake came
from a Betty Crocker box, the kind one egg
was added, and then it became scratch. She
scratched my scratched hand, and the scab
came off but it was not a scab on my hand as much
as in my ears. Ringing, ringing, my Mother's screaming.
I dive into, under, the water hold my breath until
I am forced to re-enter and hear hysteria.
I dive below again hoping it stops, and it never does.
She puts black patent leather shoes on my feet,
white socks with lace and ruffles, turns me around.
I am stiff, like a corpse, quaking.
I do not move until the clash, bang, the symbol
that it is OK to move, before I curtsey.
My cheeks, red from cortisone, steroid puffy,
stiff, and stumbling, petticoats rustling, layers of tulle lined
satin lined, elastic lined under my chin, holding
my hat on through Communion and Blessings.

****

I am holding on.
There is no other sibling. The doctors look at me
       as if that is my fault, it might as well be.
No other to look after her, whose dreams
       changed and faded a red sky morning
       only to look and tell what the night before might have held.
Maybe it is I who needs the happy pills, the elixirs
       to cure the quaking inside my stomach each time
I get the phone call to stop, remain. Still I come running
       give her oxygen, count blessings that it is not you,
       dreading the time when it may be you.
I look away every time that needle is inserted into delicate
       freckled, thin skin, watching the blood spurt out,
       up and hating every time someone says
       your mother, she's so nice, she's so loving.
       If they only knew that loving was controlling.
I wait, remain controlled, hearing the latest diagnosis.

I stand waiting for the dancing to stop.
The great aunts are lined against a wall, linear.
Their hair all the same height, their hands folded
       across their laps, their laps lined flatly,
       tucked in firmly by girdles and corsets.
My mother takes my hand, hurries, jerking, twirling
       me around, and I land on a great aunt's
       black laced shoe. Petticoats exposed, panties exposed
       showing quality of make, brand.
I have been exposed, branded perfect, each hair in place,
       loving put in place, better than the cousins' hair in place.
My mother put my hair in place. It is that picture,
       the one you cannot stand, the one in which we all stand.
My mother and her sisters, my father, my uncles,
       my grandmother, my grandfather, my cousins
       all six of them, and me, and you say you
       have never seen a group of less happy people,
       and the youngest cousin, he's squirming.
I can tell even now though it was over 45 years ago,
       squirming afraid of a belted earthquake crack.
I am looking through the crack, the one not in the picture,
       the one between the closed blinds, looking out to white sand,
       ocean, feeling the coming tidal wave crashing.

****

Travel

Moxie Peng

Sometimes I feel a kind of lightness
when I think that I breathe in the same air
that you breathe out.

Sometimes I get worried
when you are far
and your breath has to
travel through
water, forests
lands and air to
reach me.

What if
it got lost
on the way here.

New York Subway
Moxie Peng

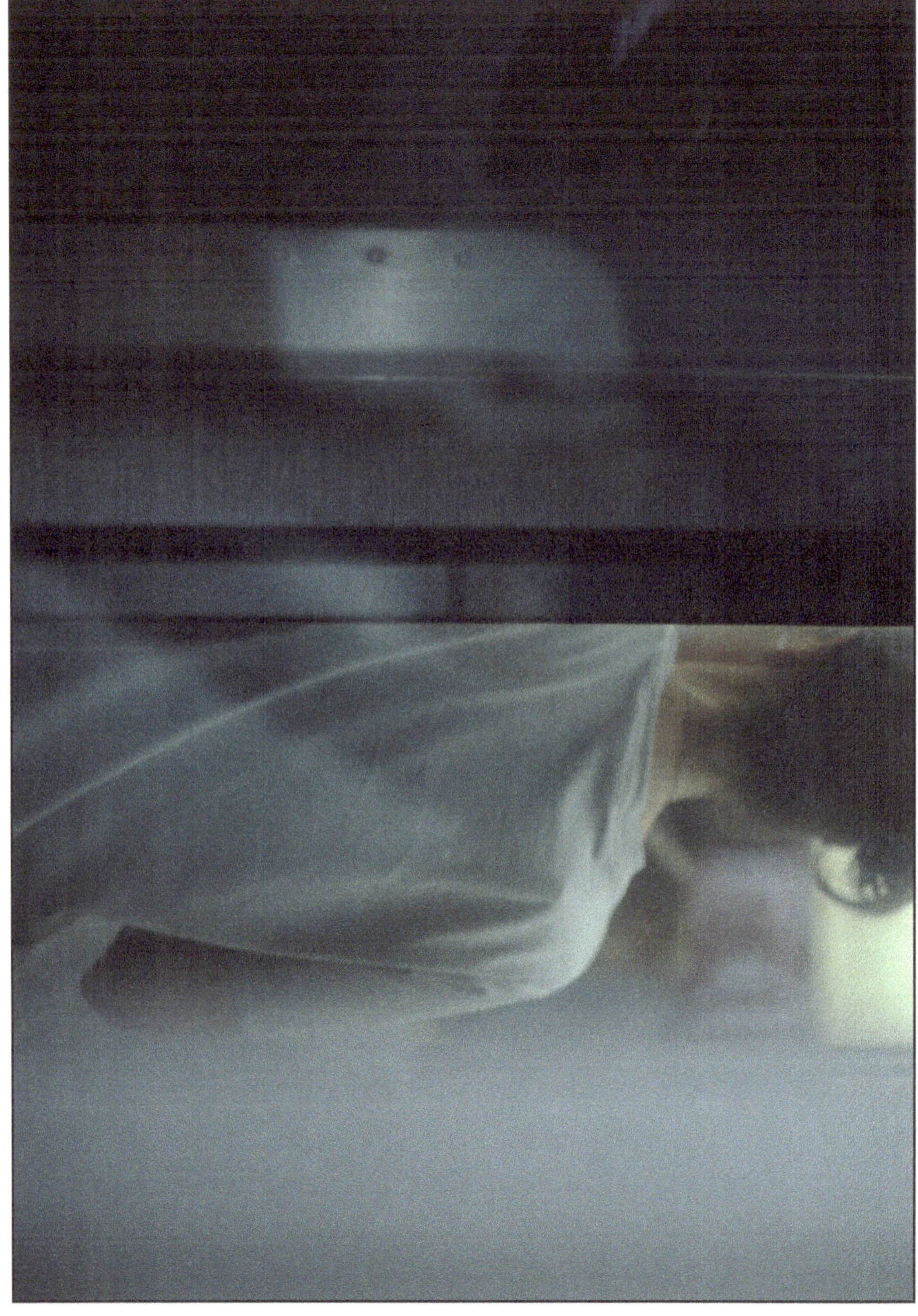

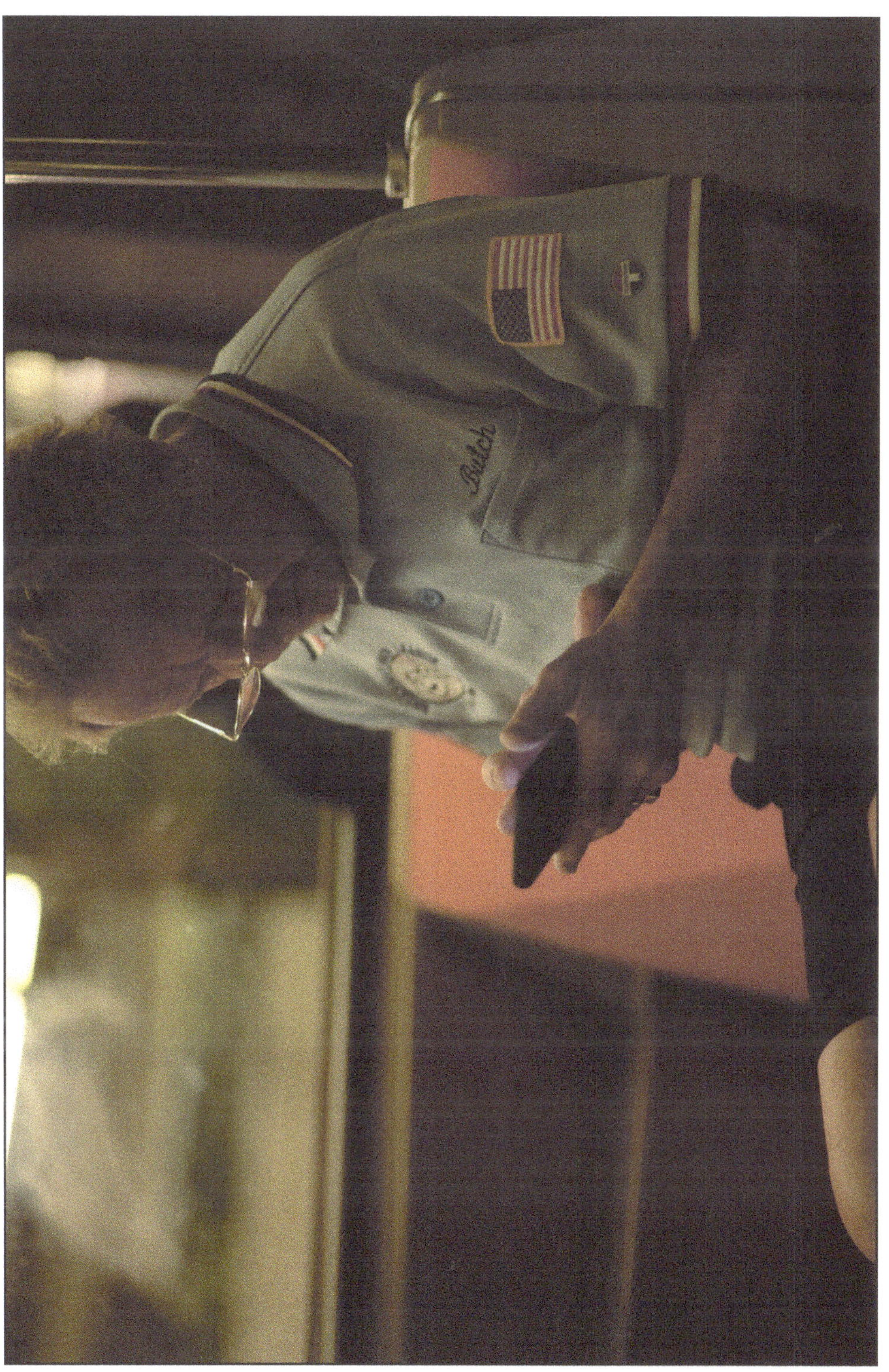

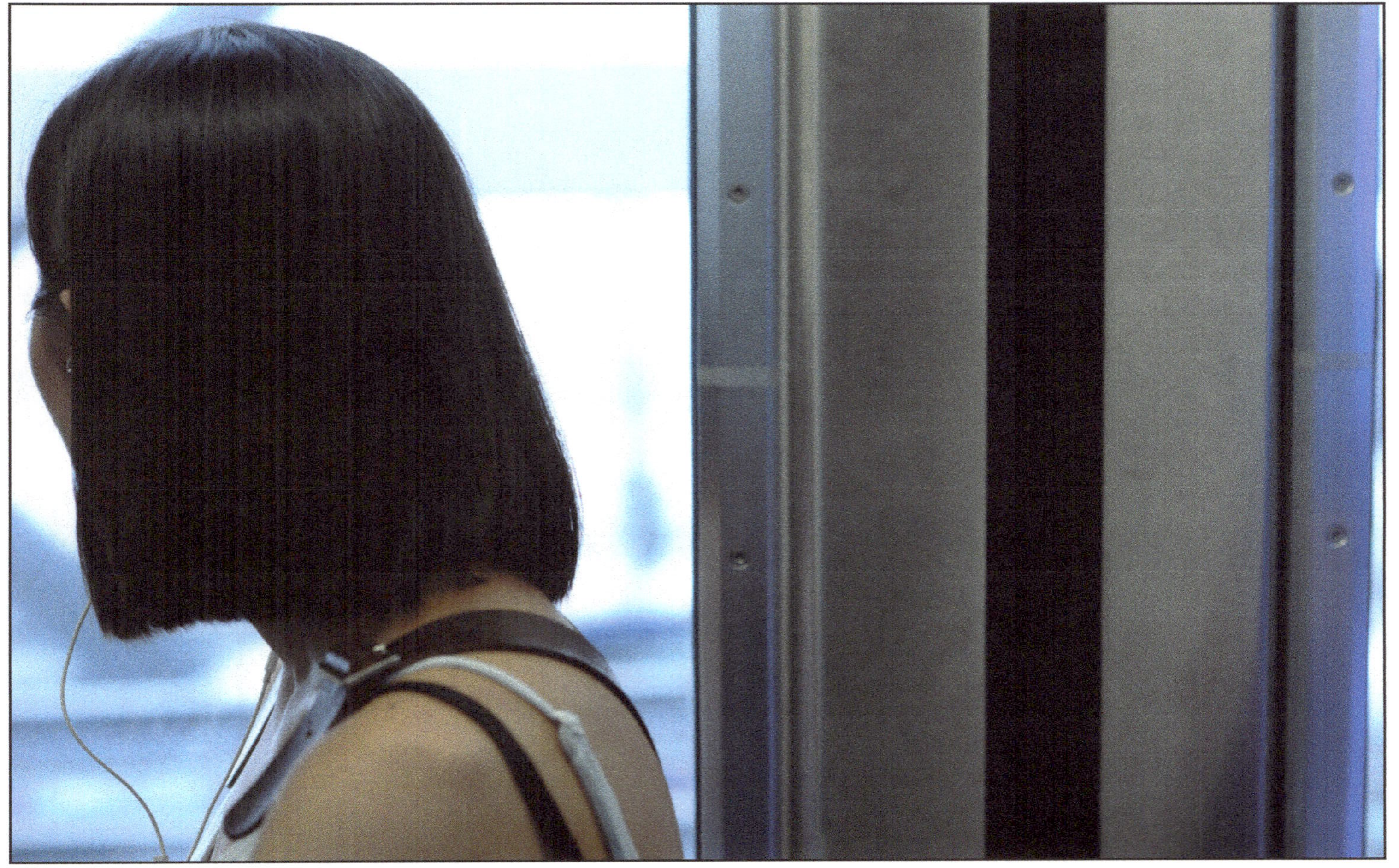

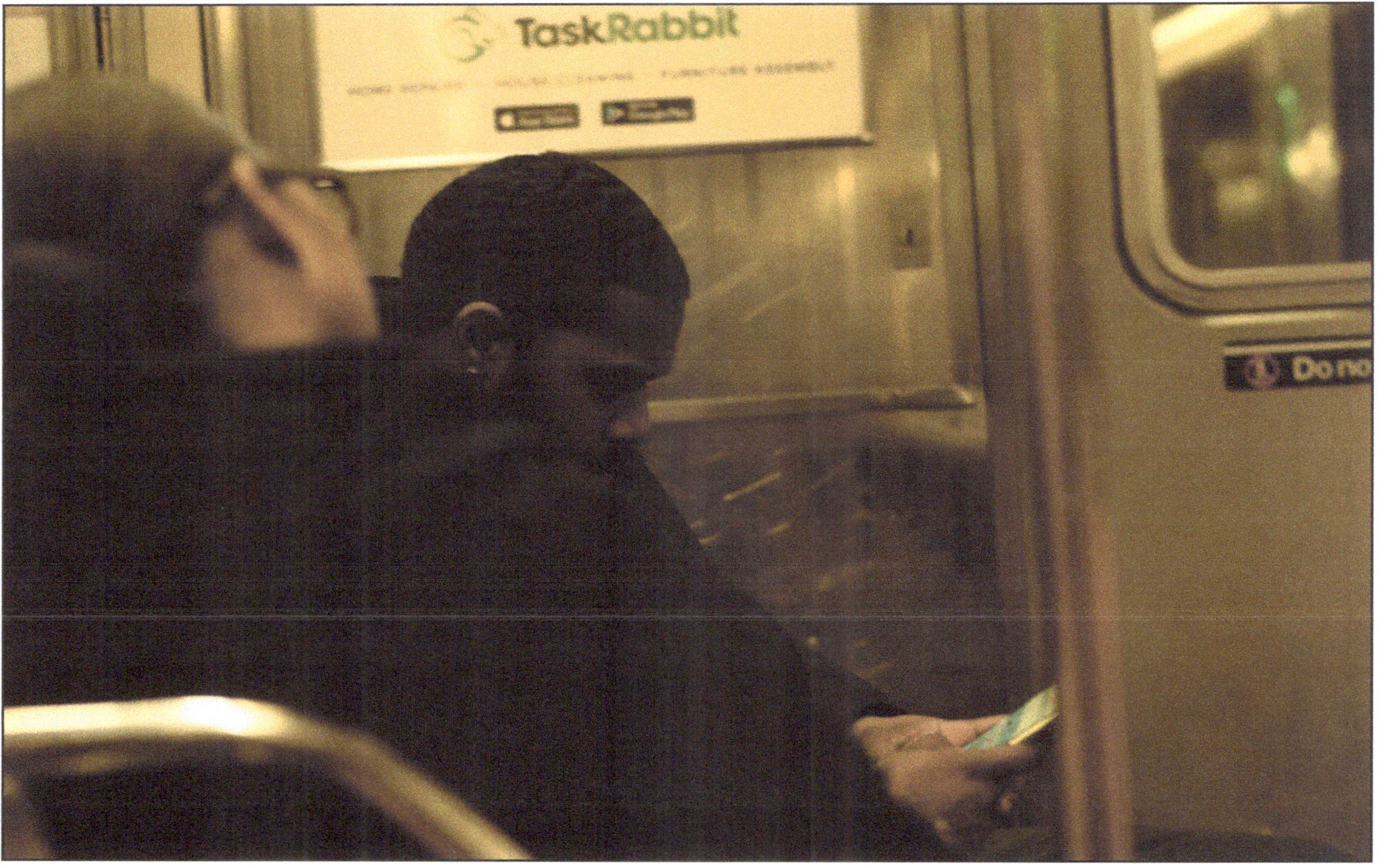
TaskRabbit
HOME REPAIRS   HOUSE CLEANING   FURNITURE ASSEMBLY
Do no

Why do Americans travel?

Antonio Fusco

Paris, May 11, 2019

Why do Americans travel?
Why do American voices travel?
Drifting across the *terrase*
an invasion
of sunshine

      — Oh! My! Gawd!

      — Hashtag!

      — Yeah, yeah.

      — Don't even get me started!

      — I want to talk about, like...

And whinging about smoking.
They don't like the smell.
I see. An aesthetic judgement.

      Well I don't like your face or your nasally tones or your endless chipper chirping or your outmoded spelling or even myself.

A bell from the 46 chimes over and over every half-second
and a horn beeps. It beeps. It does not honk.
Is it coming or going from that shithole
that is
Gare du Nord?

      Is it the pitch? The American squeak? Does it pass through the air more easily than our miserable and lumpen European mumblage that thuds in a damp bog of memory and destruction under the weight of history and the steel grey skies and the sneering and the sarcasm that drags us down into the very bowels of the earth to where we might finally find the only thing that we over here ever wanted and the only thing that could make us happy and that we long for day after day after day:

        death.

electoral college football
Robert Rubino

Hyena U. emerged victorious over Jackass State today despite being outscored 28-21.

It's the first football game played under the new so-called presidential election rule, which places a premium on quarters won rather than total points scored.

The Jackasses led 10-0 after the first quarter but the Hyenas won each of the next three quarters by one point, 7-6, thus ensuring victory under the new rule.

The Jackasses called timeout in the closing seconds with the ball on the Hyenas' one-yard line but officials voted 5-4 to let the clock run out.

"I was adamantly opposed to this ludicrous, unnecessary rule change because I feared something like this might happen," Jackass coach Jack Blockhead said. "Today the new rule clearly penalized the better team. It tears at the heart and soul of true fair-and-square American athletic competition."

Hyena U. coach Gary Grifter was, predictably, delighted with the result, and called Blockhead "a crybaby, a sore loser and a scaredy cat, and I understand he likes Cuban music and Chinese food, which tells you all you need to know about his character and credibility." And, he added, "his mother wears combat boots."

Years of social media & reality TV lobbying for the new rule claimed the old way of accumulated scoring determining the winning team un-American because it denied quarters their individual rights and reduced many to marginal status solely because they frequently weren't as populated by points.

Opponents of the rule change had said those arguments made no sense but became increasingly unable to articulate why, and eventually were reduced to maniacal screaming, exaggerated eye rolling, uncontrollable sobbing and writing letters to The New York Times.

Despite being declared the winner, an incensed Grifter insisted "the refs' blatantly blown calls accounted for all the cheating Jacksasses' points, ruining what would have been a sensational shutout, which a lot of people are saying it really was anyway."

Countered the Jackass' Blockhead: "Help! I'm being attacked by a sore winner!"

Grifter went on to call the result under the new rule "the greatest victory in football history. No, in all sports history. Ok, in all history, period, which covers a lot of time, I've been told. All right, I pronounce it the greatest victory of all time. That's more than history. That includes prehistoric, too. What, the dinosaurs are going to argue with me?"

When confronted with allegations that he or his assistants had conferred with members of the NFL champion New England Patriots for the purpose of stealing signals, deflating footballs, paying off officials or soliciting prostitutes, Grifter said: "Winning's for winners. Losing's for losers."

Ten Steps to a Unicorn Exit

Marina Hatsopoulos

With all the coverage of startups in the news, sitcoms, and movies, it's easy to learn everything you need to know about building your business by watching TV. Of course, there's no question your startup will be a so-called "unicorn," because all you need is a great idea — as certified by your best friend's enthusiasm — and the rest will take care of itself. Sure, you'll have to work, but there are always shortcuts, and the billion-dollar exit is just a meeting away.

For help and insight, find a big-name chairman who travels the world for a dozen boards, because he won't get caught up in all the details of your business. Those emails he's reading during your board meetings are with very important people who could help with an IPO. The critical thing is to take all his wisdom to heart, even if it's based on pre-historic market information, and make sure not to dilute it with your own judgment.

When it comes to strategic decisions, speed is the most important factor, so to help you with that, the following is a list of 10 ideas to blast off your startup.

1. Create buzz

Instead of wasting time with customers, who may not even use social media, focus on getting your name out there, winning awards, and producing expensive videos that have one chance in a million of going viral. Generating a PR buzz is the secret to success, plus your friends will think you've made it. Focus on your numbers: numbers of facebook friends, likes, connections on Linkedin, and how many times you're mentioned in the press. People who see all this may not be interested in buying your product, but they'll soon recognize your name.

2. Be nice

Avoid conflict so people will like you. Never make a decision that might upset someone; putting it off is more comfortable for everyone, even when that makes the problem worse in the long run. Negotiating is unseemly, and totally unnecessary, as most people are reasonable; whatever they're offering is probably fair.

3. Hire people you trust

The most loyal teams are made with friends and family — anyone you can't fire. They may not have relevant experience, but at least you won't waste time trying to find someone who does. Plus, if their performance suffers, you'll have plenty of time to get into it at parties and family dinners, where other loved ones can chime in.

4. Work hard

Capability and results are no match for a busy, frenetic office. If everybody's working 12 hours a day, progress is a sure thing. Plus, it's much more satisfying to check off all the little tasks on your To Do list than to sit back and waste time with strategic contemplation.

5. Strive for excellence

Prototypes are ugly. No matter how long it takes, make your product absolutely perfect before showing it to a customer for user feedback or test marketing. If the customers don't rave about your product when it's finally finished, that doesn't mean you're not meeting their needs; it only means they don't understand your product, but they'll get it eventually.

6. Stay positive

When you receive bad news, try to put it out of your mind as quickly as possible; no point thinking about something that's going to crush your mood. Also, always believe the engineers' forecasts on time and cost, regardless of history. The last 10 times they underestimated, they had very good reasons. This time will be different.

7. Don't tell anyone your idea -- they might try to steal it

The product development process will only get derailed and bogged down by customer input. You know best what the market needs. Plus, it's difficult and time-consuming to find customers, never mind figure out what to do with all those different opinions.

8. Don't be scared of competition

If there are already several players competing, it must be a good market. Product differentiation and innovation are nice to have, but if that doesn't work out, you can always compete on price. Nobody has ever considered trying to lower the cost of this particular product before, and commodity businesses are always the most profitable.

9. Grow as fast as possible

Don't worry about cash; it'll be there when you need it. You have more important things to worry about than the details of your financials. You're not an accountant, after all, and who cares about profitability when you're shooting for the moon. Sustainable business models are old-school. As long as your revenues are growing, M&A or IPO are a sure bet.

10. Put on a great show for investors

In your pitch, before you state in simple terms what you sell, make sure to use lots of industry acronyms. Investors may not understand, but it'll make you sound like an expert. Creating a chart with a clear comparison to the competition takes too much time and effort. As long as you have colorful diagrams showing how great your product is, and the projections show your recurring revenues skyrocketing, there's no need to quantify your value proposition. And, regardless of what business you're in, don't forget to say you're using blockchain! If investors aren't interested, don't waste time rethinking the business; just fix the pitch deck.

Remember, a great product sells itself. The reason your product will be better than that of the huge incumbents in your space with years of experience and millions to invest is because they're slow and stupid, while you're smart and nimble. After all, didn't you just win an award?

sun on roses

Photography by Hans Krueger
Poetry by Tracy Fahey

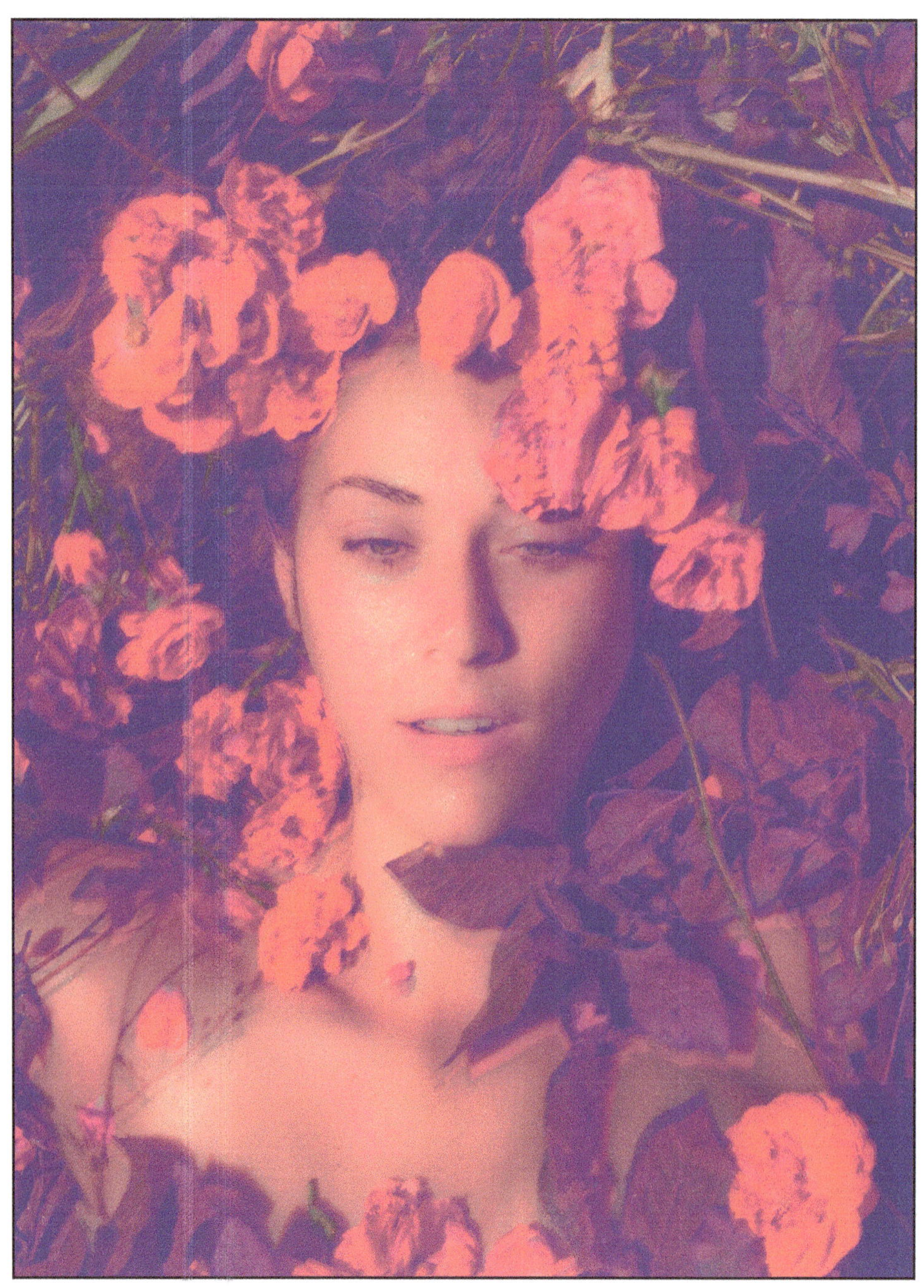

younger
i thought love would happen
naturally

lying among velvet roses
it would appear
like the sun
piercing between leaves

                                        older
                        love is an indoor game
                               without smiles

                               we sit facing
                           in darkened rooms
                         plots and counterplots
                             words like knives
                    hands clenched around dice
                               afraid to throw

somehow
the light among the leaves
has become weak and white
the jag of thorns on flesh
lacing my skin

                              i am a pale traitor

                           to that younger self
                        who dreamed sun on roses

In Order Of Appearance:

Originally from Poland, Marek Kulig grew up in New Jersey and now lives in Massachusetts, where he once taught high school English and coached basketball. He currently writes for a local food magazine and tends bar. Marek has an MA in English Literature and has contributed to a handful of writers' workshops, residencies, and programs. A member of the Network of Eastern European Writers, he's read his poetry throughout New England and the Tri-state area.

Megan is an emerging writer with a passion for 80s pop, staring at the sky, and denim. She currently lives in Seattle with two black cats that still don't know if they get along.

Kevin Morris blends together wonder and joy; nature and humanity to produce photographs which will ignite your wanderlust for Southern California beaches and nostalgic childhood memories. When he is not capturing moments on his camera, he is typically found hiking, or near the ocean with his wife and son.

Wisteria Deng graduated from the University of Michigan with a B.A. in Psychology and Creative writing. She currently lives in Boston, does clinical psychology work and writes her first book-length memoir. She is a mental health practitioner, a writer and a daughter.

Niku Rice is a birth and postpartum doula and lives in the suburbs of Detroit with her family.

Emerson DeLaCámara is a 15-year-old aspiring photographer and writer who is entering in her freshman year of high school. Growing up in a very picturesque area near the coast, photography has always been an interest of hers. She has always found a certain type of beauty in nature, taking quick pictures any chance she gets, although she had never thought about entering her photographs in contests until one day when she went to a Starbucks and saw that they had hung a customer's artwork on the wall. Since then, she has entered in multiple online photography contests on websites such as Viewbug, where she has won 29 awards, including 17 Peer Choice Awards, the Superbs Composition Award, the Community Choice Award, the Great Shot Award, the Top Class Award, and the award for Outstanding Creativity.

Lizz Ehrenpreis is a multimedia visual and graphic artist who works in hybrid and traditional forms. Her work includes themes of feminism, mental health, femininity, rage, trauma, nature, tones and gradations, pop art, queer elements, and other beautiful ephemera. Lizz studied at the Brooks Institute of Photography, and is primarily self-taught. Her work can be found on canvas, in print, online, and on denim. Her recent passion is for translating street art-style icons and imagery to fabric in her popular Jacket Off project, and was recently featured in Fused Creative's show, THE FEMININE ERA. Lizz can be found on Instagram: @thescreamingdoodle and @lzehphoto. Her portfolio and current projects are available at bestingbetty.com. Lizz can be found working and playing in Portland, Oregon, where she drinks an appalling amount of seltzer and hangs with her cats.

A. Pikovsky is a poet living in Philadelphia who has been writing poetry since childhood. She is the daughter of immigrants and the first in her family to be born in America. Her works cover many topics ranging from psychology to politics, but she always pulls from her experiences and observations as a queer, intersectional feminist.

Jodie filan is 26 and from saskatoon saskatchewan. Canadian praries. What influenced her art the most was a traumatic series of events leading to crack addiction. Losing her family and friends greatly impacted her style .Her art page is www.facebook.com/Jodiefilanart , she can be found on Instagram under Jodie filan or Jodie filan artwork.

Brenna Lakeson is a queer feminist pastor and social activist living in Atlanta, GA. Born and raised in North Carolina, she has a BA in Music from Elon University, with minors in Spanish and Latin American studies. She has an MDiv from Candler School of Theology at Emory University with particular interests in feminist theology, Hebrew Bible, and apocalyptic literature. Her writing strives to hold the stories of the marginalized in the light, create meaning from her experiences, and heal the things that hurt. Her recently published pieces can be found in Lifevest Literary Magazine at lifevestlit.com, Z Publishing's Georgia's Emerging Writers: An Anthology of Nonfiction, and America's Emerging Poets 2018: Southeast Region. Her newest endeavor, unguarded, serves to relinquish perfectionism, witness the messiness of living, and tell her full truths. Brenna's writing and blog can be found at brennalakeson.com.

Laura Lee is a Chicago area poet, college instructor, literacy tutor, and writer. Her poetry, fiction, and nonfiction have been published in print and online journals in the US, the UK, New Zealand, India, and Greece. For a complete list of publications, visit her website at: http://lauraleewriterpoet-educator.com.

Tia Harestad is a writer and artist living in Philadelphia. Born in Seattle, she graduated from the Creative Writing program at the University of Washington in 2015 and received her Master's in Fine Arts from Pacific Lutheran University in 2018. She is 25.

Josie Emmons Turner lives in Tacoma, Washington and is Tacoma's former Poet Laureate. She is the editor of the chapbook "Sarasvati Takes Pegasus as Her Mount" and her work has appeared in California Quarterly, Floating Bridge Review, Creative Colloquy, in Tahoma's Shadow and other journals. She teaches poetry and literature to seniors at Clover Park High School and earned her MFA from the Rainier Writing Workshop at Pacific Lutheran University.

Moxie Peng is a filmmaker, photographer and poet from Hunan, China. His fiction films have been selected to show at film festivals around the world. He used to work with Ren Hang in Beijing and is inspired by Ren as a photographer and a poet. He takes photos of ordinary people and the atmosphere that's created by people, space, objects and geometry. As a queer artist from China, Moxie's films are often the farmers and workers in modern China, immigrant ethnic minorities in the world, and the folks in the queer community and he often addresses intersectionalities between them. Currently, Moxie is living between Beijing and New York and planning to graduate from the Filmmaking MFA program at NYU in 2020.

Antonio Fusco is a writer living in Paris.

Robert Eugene Rubino has published poetry and prose in The Esthetic Apostle, Cagibi, The Write Launch, Hippocampus and Elysian Fields Quarterly. For more than thirty years he was a daily copy editor and weekly columnist at various California newspapers. He's old enough to have seen Willie Mays play centerfield at the Polo Grounds and smart enough to nail the New York Times crossword puzzle each Monday (other days not so much). He lives in Palo Alto, California.

Marina's writing has been published in Antioch Review, Bellevue Literary, Crab Orchard Review, F(r) iction by Tethered by Letters, The Write Launch, Pooled Ink: NCW Contest Winners, and numerous other literary journals. Marina's work has been winner or finalist in the F(r)iction Short Story Contest, the PNWA literary contest, the Jack Dyer Fiction Prize, the Prolitzer Prize and the Glimmer Train Short Story Award for new writers.Marina was Co-Founder/CEO of Z Corporation, an early leader in 3D printing out of MIT.

Hans Krueger works in the medium of photography but also constructs the sets and designs the make up and hair his friends featured in his art. His work reflects the relationship between humans and their connection to the plant and animal kingdom.

Tracy Fahey is an Irish writer. In 2017, her debut collection The Unheimlich Manoeuvre was shortlisted for a British Fantasy Award. Two of her short stories were longlisted by Ellen Datlow for Honourable Mentions in The Best Horror of the Year Volume 8. She is published in over twenty Irish, US and UK anthologies and her work has been reviewed in the Times Literary Supplement. Her first novel, The Girl in the Fort, was released by Fox Spirit Press in 2017. Her second collection, New Music For Old Rituals, was published in 2018 by Black Shuck Books.

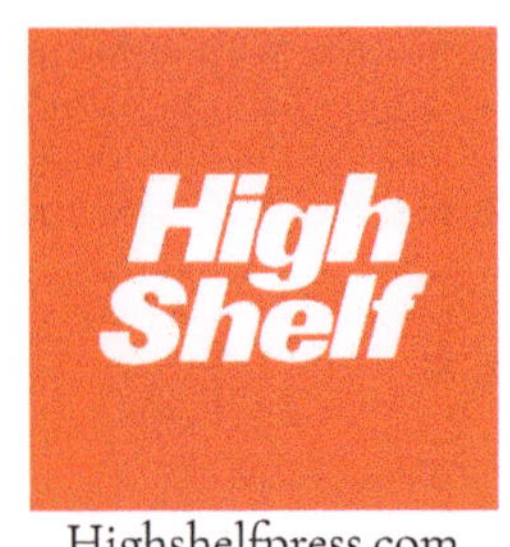

Highshelfpress.com

www.ingramcontent.com/pod-product-compliance
Lightning Source LLC
Chambersburg PA
CBHW050017040726

47599CB00014B/1429